A Letter to My Children and the Children of the World to Come

Raoul Vaneigem

Translated by Donald Nicholson-Smith

A Letter to My Children and the Children of the World to Come
Raoul Vaneigem

Originally published as *Lettre à mes enfants et aux enfants du monde à venir* by
Le Cherche Midi © 2012

English translation © 2019 by Donald Nicholson-Smith
Afterword © 2019 by John Holloway
This edition © PM Press 2019

ISBN: 978–1–62963–512–5
Library of Congress Control Number: 2017964743

Cover by John Yates / www.stealworks.com
Interior design by briandesign

10 9 8 7 6 5 4 3 2 1

PM Press
PO Box 23912
Oakland, CA 94623
www.pmpress.org

Printed in the USA by the Employee Owners of Thomson-Shore in Dexter,
Michigan. www.thomsonshore.com

For Ariane, Ariel, Chiara, Tristan, Garance,
Renaud, Sasha, Lunta

We need but one thing:
the deep joy of life.
Let its poetic power awaken and reveal itself
and everything else will be given us.

Contents

Preface to the English-Language Edition

The Consciousness of Life May Slumber but It Never Dies

The democratic election that has just installed an individual with alarming mental shortcomings in the presidency of the United States is but one example among others of the slow-motion collapse of the socioeconomic system that prevails everywhere. The sinister scythe of the multinational corporations delivers up the planet to plunder, accelerates immiseration, threatens the very survival of populations, and devastates animal, vegetable and mineral resources, which fall prey to greed and the religion of money.

Why should we be surprised if everyday life and its human consciousness are smothered and stultified by the totalitarian rule of the economy? Or if the dismay and despair so relentlessly nurtured by the international of profit and by the words that serve it end up by creating submissive hordes to whom idiocy and heedless apathy offer a sort of consolation?

The great dictatorships of the past were not blind to this phenomenon and excelled at profiting from it. In the day of a Hitler, a Stalin, a Mao or a Franco, however, the development of capitalism and the social benefits it promised lent a degree of plausibility to the notion of a supreme guide with the authority to sacrifice the present on the bloody altar of happiness to come. Now that capitalism has lost its dynamism and invests the income it hurriedly reaps from its ravages in purely financial speculation, the stagnation into which it has sunk no longer has the slightest chance of providing an apprentice dictator with the strategic opportunities once furnished by state or private capitalism, a portion of whose profits ended up improving working conditions and boosting social gains.

Populism is the product of the bastardization of Nazism and Stalinism. The class consciousness of the proletariat had already been roundly crippled by trade-union and political bureaucracy by the time the great consumerist colonization brought the solvent power of the market of false well-being to bear on the remains of all the intelligence and combativity that the workers' movement had developed and honed in its struggles before capitalism abandoned the realm of production for the now far more profitable realm of consumption.

The proletariat has now regressed to a stage earlier than the one it reached by virtue of class consciousness. It has once more become that *plebs* which from antiquity to the French Revolution constituted a conglomeration of the exploited, the roiling and dangerous mass of the poor, trapped between servility and doomed revolt. Serviceable and manipulable at will, this new *plebs* is the hotbed where the populist tribunes foster their ambitions and satisfy their appetite for domination. Historical conditions no longer allow them to exercise power over the world, so they have no recourse but to cultivate their personal power. Chaos and stagnation are their armor and their arms. They are maggots on the corpse of the old world, which is dead but continues to rot. Nothing more. But this nothing is good enough for them, for they know that ahead of them there is nothing. And so will things remain so long as we make no effort to build the new world to which millions of human beings nevertheless aspire. This we know for sure.

I have been rebuked for harboring illusions about the insurrections that recently shook the Arab world in the name of freedom. True, those uprisings have subsided, but you do not need a great mind to realize that they will surely recur.

By striking a mortal blow against absolute monarchy, against the God that served as its guarantor and against the agrarian economy that undergirded it, the French Revolution and its Enlightenment restored to men and women the right to become human beings. The end of the mandate of heaven gave them back an earth and a life that had been stolen from them and that it behooved them to enhance.

It took hardly any time, however, for free trade, which by virtue of the free circulation of persons and goods had revived hopes of emancipation, to turn into a new tyranny, a new prison.

Once heard, though, the song of freedom is never forgotten. No eclipse can extinguish the sun of consciousness.

Having experienced every form of government, what remains of life and sensitive intelligence in women and men must inevitably find its way through the ruins. In opposition to the predatory behavior that rules that social jungle where, from the ancient world to this day, we have been locked in continual strife, we have no healthy choice but to initiate, on the basis of the autonomy of all, a project aiming in solidarity to renew the forces of life and form a new alliance with nature, a project that will eradicate from the planet the international of profit and the totalitarianism of the economy which are at present laying it waste.

R.V., Brussels, February 4, 2017

Preamble

How could I address my daughters, my sons, my grandchildren and great-grandchildren, without including all the others who precipitated into the sordid universe of money and power, are at risk, even tomorrow, of being deprived of the promise of a life that is undeniably offered at birth as a gift with nothing expected in return?

Were I not repulsed by moral injunctions, I might have confined myself to high-minded humanistic declarations. It is rather inconsistent, though, to broadcast otherworldly good intentions without any warning about the monsters of everyday violence that will gobble them up in an instant.

The simplicity of man and the world man strives to live in is appearance only. The surface of beings and things has the deceptive tranquility of a lake, where dawdling fish are soon caught. What is more, the evolution of manners and attitudes is now so rapid that new light has pierced the obscurity of earlier times and exposed unheard-of pockets of manifest truth.

You may agree with a reproach that is often directed at me, namely that I write in a style requiring more effort and attention than a novel, for example.

But what is more stupidly intelligible than the rehearsal of prejudices that for centuries have done duty for thought, all the platitudes relentlessly chewed over from one generation to the next until they acquire the standing of eternal truths? Philosophies, religions and ideologies have never done anything but rubber-stamp behavior which, as varied as it may be, is always governed by supposedly unchangeable motives: the taste for power, the appeal of money, competition, the combat between force and cunning, the repression and unleashing of bestiality, a distorted form of love, guilt-ridden anxiety, the exile of the self, existential malaise, and so on.

Those whose thinking never gets beyond the simple identification of such perennial motivations, beyond tireless rumination after the fashion of ancient man, are the very same people who accuse me of repetitiveness whenever I throw a few grains of sand into the gears of a mechanical destiny which (as they well know) leads them only where they wish not to go.

The rock-hard assumptions of the past cannot be demolished without the hammer of ideas capable of pulverizing old banalities and offering the future pathways that it will in turn render banal.

But how am I to avoid putting readers off by bombarding them with burning truths which their habituation to cold ashes makes them loath to embrace? I have no wish to resort to the kind of literary devices writers use to seduce their audience. My challenge is how to eschew the artifices of seduction while simultaneously remaining loyal to an idleness that I rate highly enough to practice its virtues.

Leonardo da Vinci is said to have covered the walls of a room with little mirrors. He would settle down there to muse at the center of a microcosmos that "reflected" him by repeating and varying his image. He remained seated amid this host of reflections whose implications he alone drew. Are we not all at every moment surrounded by a mosaic of disparate elements among which the same things and the same beings continually return, but always under a different aspect which alters their lighting and endows them with new meanings?

The repetition here is only apparent. Think of musical variations on a particular theme. When, at the end of a piece, the composer repeats the opening theme, its constancy will have been enhanced by all the successive improvisations to which it has given rise in the meantime.

Mosaic composition plays on the paradoxical presence of both familiarity and distance. It is up to readers to refocus on themselves so as to disentangle from my writing what echoes their own aspirations and to guess down which pathways to possible fulfillment their labyrinthine desires lead.

Do you squander your energy working at what merely dries you up and impoverishes you? Do you balk at the effort required by engagement with the world and by the will to transform it from top to bottom? True, it is far more comfortable to endorse the aberrant ruling system than to champion authentic life, but I refuse to make this easier but cowardly choice, just as I refuse to give rotten and hateful emotions the right to smother the human consciousness of a life yet to be constructed.

So conditioned are we by the guidelines with which everyday survival punctuates its dismal trajectory that flashes of life in all its gratuity frighten us with their unprecedented clarity and deeply offend our commonsensical convictions.

I do not care, however, to turn away from the difficult but exhilarating route that carries me to and fro between what I am and what I want to be. My way goes up and down, always the same, yet ever-changing, as my feet tread, dig and furrow it.

In the depths of the apparent obscurity of words and phrases in which we seem lost, there always comes a moment hospitable to life's awakening. It will arise from the existential magma we are wading through, springing forth as though on the lookout for an unanticipated encounter.

This kind of confrontation with oneself restores significance and simplicity to what has seemed complex.

Consciousness is enriched by what one already possesses. The best cure for that failure to live that I have called survival sickness is the discovery of one's own wealth as measured in gratification, creativity, love, and the wild desire to free oneself from the oppression of the commodity.

The "word" must be given the time to descend from the head into the body, where other ears hear and record it after their fashion, where the language of the emotions distil it before calling upon a consciousness with its origins in our mental activity which is the vector of the weight and grace of what is human, ever more human.

How many days, how many years it takes for "meaning to be embodied" in the word! How long before we refine our emotional bestiality instead of repressing it or unleashing it down the byways of barbarism, as prescribed by the lengthy past of our inhumanity!

I call for nothing less than the sovereignty of life. I have no interest in preaching or prophesying. My thoughts are reiterated, yet they progress step by step, for the call is continual. My idleness is a gamble on a resonance effect whereby echoes will be relayed everywhere without any further effort being required. By playing on the near and the far, I distance and precede myself at the same time. I find devious ways of extricating myself unscathed from the sinking sands of survival. My approach runs counter to the vain struggles of those who flail about desperately only to be swallowed up by a fatalism, a bitter lucidity where they macerate like corpses.

If you ask what is the closest to my heart, my answer is the song of the earth whose opening theme, as in the case of the aforementioned musical variations, is identical to the final one. My deepest wish is to help lay the groundwork for a society where my happiness, that of my children, my lover, my loves of old, my friends, and of all those for whom I feel affection is intimately linked to the happiness of every human creature laid low in this world by the tyranny of money, power, and commodities. That goes too for the beasts, not least the beast within us. Between the alpha and omega of my intentions lies nothing but the attempt and the temptation to demonstrate the well-foundedness of this choice of mine.

A Change in Civilization Is Taking Place before Your Eyes

You are privileged to have been born at a crucial moment in history. A period when everything is being transformed and nothing will ever be the same again.

The opportunity is unprecedented, but seizing it is daunting, for, as beneficial as it may be in prospect, every change is accompanied by uncertainties, gropings in the dark and missteps. Its fragility exposes it to a confusion that may erode its merits.

On your shoulders still lies the weight of an inhuman past. A past that I fancy I am not alone in wishing to be done with. In the merciless struggle between the old and the new, you have landed right in the middle of the battlefield.

One civilization is collapsing and another is being born. The misfortune of inheriting a planet in ruins is offset by the incomparable joy of witnessing the gradual advent of a society such as history has never known—save in the shape of the mad hope, embraced by thousands of generations, of someday leading a life at last freed from poverty, barbarity and fear.

We were despairing of ever achieving what was commonly deemed a mirage, a utopia, but suddenly its reality is now taking shape before our very eyes.

Little by little a new society is emerging from the mist. For the time being it is no more than a rough sketch, with the best intentions rubbing shoulders with the worst. But you are not only faced by a formless block which you are expected to carve into a living, harmonious sculpture: you are yourselves part of that block.

Before you lies experience that is oddly both solitary and collective: you will each be alone in plunging into it, yet many others will be at your side, likewise busy "sculpting their own existence."

Could there be anything more apt for a human being than combining with others to construct our own happiness along with that of all? From this passionate adventure you will quickly learn three lessons: (1) what is wished for from the bottom of the heart has every chance of coming about; (2) nothing is ever definitively won; and so (3) beware of pride and presumption!

The Old Nightmares Still Disturb Our Dreams of Renewal

Let me say a word about the past that burdens me, the future that exhilarates me, and the present in which at every moment a reality I consider intolerable clashes with the living reality to which I aspire.

One need only review the roughly ten thousand years that make up our history to realize what a gulf separates technological from cultural progress. The path from the neolithic forge to the nuclear plant is immeasurably long; that from the sacking of the first city-states some six thousand years before our era and the Nazi camps, the Soviet gulag or the Rwandan genocide is *horrifyingly* short. From the bronze dagger to the ICBM, the military monster has barely altered.

What weight do technological advances and magnificent art carry alongside the poverty and fear whose permanence seems to reduce the long plaint of suffering humanity to a vain cry?

How can we forget that while Bach's genius was enriching world culture millions of wretches were starving, dying under torture or being massacred by the armies of princes and the laws of the powerful?

I lived in a world where the yoke of tradition obliged you to bow down. Woe unto anyone who dared to stand up and mark themselves off from the enslaved masses! Force, lies and cunning were deployed to persuade them with carrot and stick to get back in line, to rejoin the herd that the power of State, church, and ideologies of every stripe were leading to the slaughterhouse.

Children were then taught that society was divided into two camps: those who eat and those who are eaten. From the tenderest age you were supposed to fight. For whom? For what? The noblest and the most ignominious of pretexts were wheeled out in order to lead us astray into battles that were not ours. In fighting others, we were actually fighting ourselves, unaware for the most part of the evil with respect to which we were at once victims and accessories.

The crime that a mercenary civilization has hitherto perpetrated against childhood is to have set predation above sensitivity and generosity of spirit.

Life as an individual and social adventure was so relentlessly hedged about with obstacles, disillusion and dashed hopes that even rare and wondrous moments of happiness were overwhelmed by cynical mockery born of bitterness and resentment.

Instead of devising a destiny for themselves capable of fulfilling their longing for enfranchisement, servile masses submitted to leaders, elected or self-appointed, who promised them a better life even as they condemned them to poverty and death. Their differences notwithstanding, such sinister figureheads as Hitler, Dollfuss, Lenin, Trotsky, Stalin, Mussolini, Franco or Mao Zedong were frequently set up as models of everyday behavior. They were, in effect, merely inflated projections of the solid family men and petty office managers who swarm around us like maggots.

The Earthquake of the French Revolution

All the same, more than two centuries ago an economic, political and social earthquake overturned the form and structure of a world with foundations so old that it seemed to embody the plan of an eternal God. We now know that the Supreme Being—a veritable succubus battening on humanity—was a fraud perpetrated by priests and princes that was meant to lend an ineffable character to the order of social precedence and regulate the status of masters and slaves.

The French Revolution put an end to an economy based for nearly seven thousand years on agriculture and the appropriation of land. God died on the scaffold along with the hapless Louis XVI, destroyed as the symbol that he embodied. The twin peaks of the monarchic and divine principle—crown of a hierarchical pyramid whose cohesion was the guarantor of an unshakeable tyranny—were thus chopped off. Once deprived of the sacrosanctity of its summit, the decapitated pyramid was bound to collapse, no matter how hard ideological dictatorships from Robespierre to Mao might strive to restore its unified and mythical structure.

The fall of the ancien régime and the rejection of its monarchic and religious totalitarianism signaled the triumph of the ideas of liberty, equality and fraternity. Thanks to the Revolution of 1789 the thinking of the Encylopedists—the Diderots, d'Alemberts, D'Holbachs, Chamforts, Rousseaus,

Voltaires, and Mesliers—achieved concrete form and fueled the project of moving from dream to reality.

The hope of achieving a genuinely human life aroused a collective fervor never before seen in history. For the first time, perhaps, human beings sensed that living is not the same thing as surviving and that any existence worth the name does not consist in scrabbling for subsistence day after day like the birds, who as Louis Scutenaire says, "eat only in great fear."

Survival is indeed the concern of the animal and not the human world.

The False Promise of Free Trade

Much as religious obscurantism, narrow-mindedness, and prohibitions on free thinking arose from the economic and social stagnation inherent to the structure of agrarian enclosure, so the Declaration of the Rights of Man was largely the product of an economic innovation, namely the free circulation of goods and persons that marked the absolute victory of the bourgeoisie over aristocratic tyranny.

What happened then? The answer is that free trade, which had promised the inauguration of a free life, swiftly turned that dream into a nightmare.

It very soon became apparent that the freedom granted to trade handed profit and the avaricious spirit of "enrich yourselves" the power to reject, prohibit or hollow out the very human rights that it had helped establish.

As of 1792, the two rival factions of revolutionary power both bent their efforts to this task, each after its own fashion. The liberal Girondists had no problem conflating human and commercial liberty. And as for the statism of Robespierre and the Jacobins, liberty was the grease they used to lubricate the guillotine. Let us remember Manon Phlipon's cry: "Oh Liberty, what crimes are committed in your name!" Nor should we forget that Olympe de Gouges was beheaded for calling for equality between woman and man.

Capitalism's victory over the agrarian economy made the "captain of industry" the model of the new man—a Prometheus whose dynamism and technical genius were supposed to steer society toward well-being. But no sooner had capitalism smashed the shell of an archaic economy than it emerged in its turn as a hermetic structure, an immutable world where all change was confined to an enclosed field strictly hedged about by the quest for profit and the repression of whatever hindered that quest. Those who had rid themselves of agrarian despotism now found themselves under the heel of financial tyranny.

To justify the exploitation of the proletariat, industrial capitalism propagated an ideology of technical and social progress cynically identified with a frenetic growth of profit accruing to the owner class. A battery of laws favoring the freedom to enrich oneself and the destruction of a freedom to live, the cries of which had to be gagged.

From Productivism to Consumerism

The drive to maximize profit has always governed the development of capitalism. It was what gradually replaced the coerced obligation to produce with the no less imperative duty to consume. Whereas the production of goods and the extraction of raw materials had since the nineteenth century constituted the main sector of the economy and the chief source of revenue, the 1950s saw the emergence of a new emphasis that precipitated a considerable disordering of customs and attitudes.

The necessity of production had created a working class whose intensive labor and wretched wages enriched the bosses and the bourgeoisie. These new slaves differed from serfs under the ancien régime in but one respect: their growing consciousness of the unjust fate that condemned them to poverty even as they produced the wealth of a nation. In consequence they arrogated to themselves the right to contest the bourgeoisie's lies and oppression. They felt that they had a historical mission in the sense that their emancipation would entail the end of class society and lay the foundations of an egalitarian regime.

To arm itself, the working class drew on the same Enlightenment philosophy which had helped the bourgeoisie overthrow the tyranny of the ancien régime and proceed to set up its own despotism. The authoritarian and patriarchal power of the monarchist and theocratic order against which thinkers of bourgeois background had rebelled was thus encountered by the proletariat in a secularized form, divested of God but just as ferociously repressive as ever.

The Illusion of Consumable Well-Being

The second half of the twentieth century saw the all-powerful sector of industrial production gradually give ground to consumption. The very survival of capitalism depended on this new emphasis.

The fact was that the uprising of colonized peoples threatened to deprive the industrialized nations of their source of raw materials. How could this danger be avoided? The solution found by a so-called democratic Europe was to replace the exploitation of rebellious colonies by the colonization of their own toiling masses, an option that had the distinct advantage of requiring no recourse to force.

The proletarians of the colonialist nations were thus invited to a feast of false pretenses: the worldwide banquet of generalized consumption. (The United States had already successfully tried out this new form of servitude.) The exploited soon got used to adopting the dress of consumers as soon as they doffed their work overalls or white collars.

It would take some time, however, for it to dawn on them that by leaving one factory where they were subjected to the constraints of production and entering another where the seduction of consumable goods relieved them of their wages, they were being doubly exploited.

The capitalists won on two fronts: on the one hand, their profits suffered less from the workers' incessant strikes and demands, while, on the other, the access of the majority to consumer goods hitherto reserved for the bourgeoisie disarmed the proletariat by surreptitiously inciting it to work in order to consume more. That class's new standing—easily mistaken for a promotion to the bourgeoisie—eventually succeeded in devastating class consciousness and causing the workers to forget the very term "proletarian."

A class, however, is defined by being, not having. The bourgeoisie is in this sense a mongrel class, the only class that tends to reduce its being to having. For the aristocracy being is simply the privilege of birth, the risible basis of an odious tyranny. The being of the proletariat is an "obligation to become," a being that strives to abolish classes, beginning with its own, by identifying itself with that movement of "being" which overturns the hegemony of "having."

Consumerism Has Reduced All Values to Market Value

The shift from productivism to consumerism had a truly seismic effect on a world hitherto ruled by constraints, authority, hierarchy and respect for religious and ideological values.

The power of the bosses was essential for the imposition of production norms. It eroded slowly but surely in favor of a democracy of the supermarket according to which individual choice prevailed without any limits save one, namely the obligation to pay for "freely chosen" purchases.

Persuading people to do whatever makes them happy had one great merit: it sold things. The advertising media set about hyping the indispensability of a host of harmful, mediocre and useless products. Relentless harrying subjected the ear, even the subconscious, to a sort of raucous waltz designed to substitute a gamut of false needs and artificial desires for the melodies of an authentic life unmoved by the oompahs of fake brass bands.

On the other hand, the illusion of individual free choice added attractive colors to the ideology of pleasure billed as hedonism. Consumerism threw overboard all the ethical and religious scruples that had smothered sensual appetites under the weight of sin and guilt. Even the ancient virtue of sacrifice, preached for centuries, now found itself in grave jeopardy.

This economic new wave also encouraged—though quite unintentionally—a critique of work, to which the bourgeoisie had dedicated a veritable cult. The moral virtue of toil and its celebration lost much of its credibility when it became clear that the chief thing work could buy was happiness on the installment plan.

Consumerism has altered age-old behavior. The liberation of women and children, concern for animals, and respect for nature have all proved fertile fields for the development of new, profitable commodities susceptible of sensitizing consumers to the welfare of babies, young girls, and dogs.

The Revolution of Everyday Life

Not until the uprising of May 1968 in France was it possible to gauge the degree to which consumerism, the promise of a society of well-being and the attendant disillusionments had created favorable conditions for a genuine revolution of everyday life.

As a result of the blows struck against age-old traditions by the new economic dispensation, the young generation of the time undertook to sweep away all the values inherited from an archaic society that a modernizing bourgeoisie had adapted to its own requirements: patriarchy, hierarchy, church, army, work, sacrifice, dominance of the male, and the paterfamilias, contempt for women, children, and nature. Nothing at that moment escaped virulent criticism. Censorship was mocked. The supposed crime of blasphemy was no more, likewise the principle of lèse-majesté, the moral order in general, and respect for dignitaries ecclesiastical and secular alike.

Sad to say, whatever fails to take deep root in everyday experience and its liberatory impulses soon sinks and disappears in the morass of ordinary corruption. Of course, the purpose of the vogue for consumable freedoms was hardly the emancipation of men and women. Rather, it was governed by a slogan repeated day in and day out: "Consume! Consume whatever you want, but consume!"

Inasmuch as the exchange value of a product is more important, economically speaking, than its use value, its utility, and its quality, the logic of the market tended to reduce products and ideas formerly deemed either prestigious or worthless to the same level, thus making them interchangeable.

A true clean sweep has now eviscerated not just religious and ideological values once held to be immutable but also human ones—authenticity, solidarity, freedoms of body and consciousness—which over the generations had managed to resist the dominant oppression and lies.

Many now came to understand that dedicating their vital energies to the construction of a genuine life was preferable to squandering them on ideological and religious infighting in which blood and filth besmirched whatever risible and pathetic victories might be secured.

The notion of a life authentically lived began to make its way. It is still taking its first stumbling steps, but, no matter how obscurely, it embodies the awareness that its realization must imply the sovereignty of the living forces.

Finance Capital: Money as Mains Sewerage

At the same time, however, a regression was in the offing—transient, like all regressions, yet formidable. A new spiral in its development would make it possible once more for capitalism to apply totalitarian shackles to the will to live to which the occupations movement of May 1968 had committed itself by championing the birth of a new society and the collapse of the commodity system.

How is it that the life forces aroused in 1968 have for almost fifty years now been underground, continuing the struggle wherever the weight of despair has not succeeded in turning them against themselves and changing them into death reflexes, the drive for suicidal annihilation? The answer is that consumerist capitalism has given way to a financial capitalism that ceases to invest in business, renounces its own dynamism and derives most of its profits from stock market fluctuations.

The cyclone of financial speculation has completely razed all past values, human and inhuman alike. No belief, no idea, no behavior has resisted the monetary tide. Everything is invalidated by becoming exchangeable with anything else to the benefit of a single absolute value, namely money. A mad money that revolves around itself and devastates the planet in its frantic quest for short-term profit

The absurd dictatorship of financial trading has ushered in a mercantilism of "the last days"—an apocalyptic system whose madcap race to nothingness terrifies us and plunges our bodies and consciousness into darkness.

A sinister voice seems to boom forth in the manner of the cunning biblical prophets, firming up its hold over masses panic-stricken by the supposedly imminent end of the world. "Enjoy yourselves," the voice proclaims, "because tomorrow will be worse!" The message is fatalism, spreading a fear and resignation from which all the remnants of demagogic state power hasten to extract material and spiritual profit. Meanwhile, information distilled by media in the pay of multinational mafias works methodically to brainwash the hordes and get them crawling and writhing in a state of resigned resentment.

For and Against Culture

In former times much was made of a system of ideas, known as culture, whose inculcation was expressed in the form of ritual or profane practices. Culture ruled custom. An unstated consensus viewed it as the perfect measure of a civilization that prided itself on its religious and moral prejudices, its pacific and warlike proclivities, its knowledge, art, science, public buildings, libraries and museums.

Every schoolchild was supposed to acquire culture as a way of marking him or herself off from the ignorant rabble, meaning manual workers, whose subjugation the intellectuals were charged with ensuring, either by justifying their abject submission or by leading them by the hand toward "bright tomorrows."

By acknowledging that colonized peoples once deemed primitive did in fact possess a culture, the progressivism of the industrial age granted them a form of existence which, as though by divine grace, transcended their status as mere beasts of burden. In the pantheon of its universal imperialism, bourgeois ideology in a way assigned Dogon or Inuit culture a proletarian character, thus bestowing a dignity on the exploited class that it simultaneously withheld by reducing it to the lowest level of survival.

Culture became a weapon. It won its spurs by virtue of its response to the assault upon it by the horde of German intellectuals exalting brute force, or similarly that of academic

Maoists glorifying the exhaustion produced by manual labor and obliging students to subject themselves to it *en masse*.

Everything argues for the continued defense of culture, especially considering that in the market where slaves with doctorates pursue their deplorable careers, Shakespeare and Dante are as nothing alongside the communications techniques that make it possible to sell—and to sell oneself.

All the same, sooner or later we shall have to face culture's ambiguity, even its false pretenses, because it is ultimately nothing but a scheme for commandeering knowledge.

Culture is surely the fruit of the alienation at the root of humanity's separation from itself, of that transformation of the life force into labor force which gives rise to the division between intellectual and manual work, gives mastery over the body to the head, and places terrestrial matter under the yoke of the mind.

Being a system of thought separated from life—or, in other words, an ideology—culture is willy-nilly a tool of domination: it should therefore hardly surprise us that it carries within itself the seeds of the kind of populism that scorns it.

Culture is a confined space, a conceptual prison that must be opened. How can we be freed from its alienating power without freeing what it has trapped in its drive to domination?

Learning to live demands a vital passion: curiosity, the desire to learn, the thirst for knowledge. This vitality is gloriously evident in the child's wonderment, just as long as it is not captured and sterilized by a taste for power inculcated by a pedagogy of predation.

The desire for knowledge inhabits the child and anyone who has preserved their childhood within them. My wish is that everyone should become wise out of desire, not to satisfy a need to dominate. What greater satisfaction could there be than that felt by anyone who knows that a generous dispersal of their knowledge reaps a rich harvest.

After Master Thinkers, Unthinking Slaves

From childhood up until the threshold of maturity my education proceeded under the threat of an intellectual terrorism that passed for the touchstone of "our" European culture. Hardly less formidable than the theologians and scholiasts of the Middle Ages, philosophers and thinkers—however pertinent or important they were deemed to be—punctuated and exacted a ransom of obligatory reference all along the highways and byways of thought.

Descartes, Kant, Spinoza, Hegel, Kierkegaard, Marx, Nietzsche, Bakunin, Freud, Groddeck, Reich served us as firebombs to hurl into the thick of debates with a sense of provocation that barely concealed our wish to rout adversaries whom we judged despicable.

In complete ignorance of Adorno, Bloch and Benjamin, the hairsplitters of a Marxism rehashed by Lenin, Trotsky, Stalin or Mao confronted one another using the leading imbeciles of the day—the Sartres, de Beauvoirs and their ilk—as sticks with which to beat one another. This absurd donnybrook over political dogma raged on as the free-for-all of politico-philosophical inquisitors continued with desperate zeal to anathematize all modish "deviationist" interpretations of Marxism.

Once all this charlatanism—at once laughable and bloodthirsty (think of Stalin's trials or the Chinese Cultural Revolution)—had run its course, the doctrinal references ceased being wielded like sledgehammers. The intellectual arrogance of "Marx tells us . . ." "Freud argues that . . . ." and "Nietzsche shows that . . ." no longer produced anything but mockery.

True, there was good reason to celebrate the demolition of personages on pedestals we were supposed to venerate or scorn. Implicitly invited now, at last, to think for ourselves, were we going to discover the existential soil in which the real questions grow before being uprooted and perverted in the vast and useless realms of abstraction?

Plunging into the great world library and drawing from it, on our own initiative, the elements of human consciousness so needful for every life—was this not a way to rediscover the pleasure of learning and teaching, a pleasure at long last unburdened of the will to power that had been smothering it?

The demise of master thinkers would surely open up a vast domain to exploration by living thought. We had every opportunity now to leave the beaten paths of cultural abstraction.

Alas, the unleashing of speculation has turned the tabula rasa on which we wanted to build a new society, a new civilization, into an arid and filthy place, perfectly unfit for our hoped-for banqueting. We had expected unending festivity; what befell was full-blown devastation.

Spurred on by the totalitarian rule of money, the era of nothing, of nihilism, was upon us. A game of chess stage-managed by an idiot. No more up or down, or left and right. Everything was carried off in a maelstrom of profit sweeping all life away.

The dilapidation of the planet and the deliberate elimination of species is the true face of nothingness. Wherever profit's great reaper goes, the grass never grows again. The dictatorship of finance makes no claim to leave those who dream of sowing and fertility with anything but the sterile outrage of despair.

Religions, ideologies and beliefs have slowly been emptied of their content by a single religion, a single ideology, a single belief, namely the omnipotence of money.

The supremacy of the Spirit has not survived the rout of divine supremacy. When the gods were first torn from their pedestals and thrown to the ground, their fragments served to underpin ideologies, some of which rose to the level of genuine secular religions. But then these grand ideologies crumbled in their turn and lost all the sanctity they had filched from the churches.

All that remains today is empty thought, self-sufficient in the sense that it is detached from life. Whatever substance it is filled with, it remains empty, for its sole justification is its function: the removal of consciousness from a proxy existence rendered all the more inauthentic because it is enhanced by illusions.

The running warfare of the young generations against cultural leaders which shaped our commitments was co-opted by the commodity system in order to exalt philistinism and jettison literature, history, philosophy, the teaching of ancient Greek and everything that did not conform to the injunction "Get rich!"

The schools abandoned their vocation to impart knowledge in favor of providing their students with the weapons needed to master the market system and engage in the loathsome struggle for survival in which individuals are judged according to the likelihood of their success or failure.

Admittedly, market-based civilization has always given priority to exchange value, to the logic of money. Money smeared blood and excrement over everything it touched, but at least its appropriation allowed one to survive. The acquisition of goods provided a perverse consolation amid the woes of a joyless existence. But now that the frenzy for profit is destroying the planet and all life, money is slowly but surely heading toward its own negation. Its devaluation is no longer a rare accidental occurrence but rather the sign of its ongoing self-destruction.

Crony capitalism has its own hired intellectuals. They envisage the abolition of culture because of its high cost, because it does not serve the market and is liable to encourage the passion for knowledge that invariably tends to expose the lies of power. Obscurantism suits business.

At the same time, however, there are other intellectuals who oppose the kind of obscurantist populism that promotes a culture of mediocrity and is based on the vilest of prejudices. These are partisans of an elitist culture which must be paid for and which is restricted to the well-to-do, a culture stripped of all sinew that lies mummy-like in the sarcophagus of the spectacle.

We have strictly no use for a conflict reminiscent of Rabelais's absurd and bilious character Picrochole, always spoiling for a fight, which pits an anticultural culture against a commercial one for which knowledge is nothing but an alibi for profit. Populism and elitism alike foster ignorance. And ignorance is ever the servant of tyranny.

I want knowledge in its diversity to be accessible to all. Transcending culture means preserving it as a legacy of universal knowledge, while destroying it as a separate sphere, an ideology, a tool of power.

Let us restore full rein to the curiosity that is so alive in childhood and that would remain alive were it not diverted and corrupted by the predatory tendencies of ordinary life. For a start, let us guarantee free access to education and learning, to all conservatories and academic institutions, to reading, museums, exhibitions, concerts, operas, public lectures, conferences of experts and scholars. Let everyone share their knowledge freely so that the pleasure of learning can fuel the pleasure of teaching.

Everything should be begun again from scratch so that joy in living can see off dreary *survival*—such is the *sine qua non* of any genuine human progress. The top priority. Think of it when the day of self-managed societies comes!

Populist Regression, the Culture of Nothing, and the Dumbing Down of the Masses

The erosive effect of the profit principle renders the land barren. The injunction "Nothing is true, so everything is permitted" promotes a nihilism that is good for business, because chaos favors every kind of malversation. Speculative capitalism sells off the ruins of the past, decimating the present in the process; it oversees the promotional sale of relics and it markets dead ideas which, no matter how obviously defunct, it swiftly galvanizes and passes off as the latest thing.

The State and the multinationals exploit the fetor of fear and emotional plague to deck out in new clothes such putrefied and nauseating ideologies as patriotism, communitarianism, tribalism, neoliberalism, neocommunism, and neofascism. The business mafias offer citizens a choice between leprosy and cholera, or in other words between protection dearly paid for and a lack of protection whose perils hired killers are assigned to emphasize.

The proletariat was conscious of the struggle to be waged against the exploitation of man by man. Plebeians by contrast possess only the animal's survival instinct: their emotional blindness is governed by nothing save the power of the predator and the cunning of the prey. They withdraw into themselves in a mean-spirited fear and a resentful passion for security that interprets the presence of the Other, the foreigner, the "outsider," the different—Jew, Arab, Gypsy, homosexual, or simply the next-door neighbor—as a threat of universal annihilation.

A diffuse and fantasied terror now presides over bloody upsurges of nationalism, religious fanaticism, and puritanism, complete with its explosions of hedonism.

How to resist? How to come to grips with conservatism and bar the way to the most insufferable form of populism? None of the solutions proposed is satisfactory. We do not want a reverse violence that meets terror with terror, fear with fear and aggression with aggression. Yet we also reject humanistic hypocrisy, the bleating, mushy and bleeding-heart ideology that reduces human rights to the sort of promotional packaging that commercial interests are so good at turning to their advantage.

Once the corruption intrinsic to the cult of money had broken down the barriers between Right and Left political parties, that same corrupt system hastened to re-erect them as a way of concealing its scandalous proliferation by means of a sort of commercial *bal masqué* conducted in both camps at once. It was indeed imperative that popular anger be prevented from turning against the real agents of economic, political, social and existential disaster, namely finance capital and the multinational corporations. Attention had to be drawn away at all costs from the sight of the sneaking tentacles put out everywhere by the market and by financial speculation. It falls to the communications media, tried and tested by the advertising industry, to divert this anger, to redirect it onto scapegoats and to fuel absurd contests between good and evil—two perfectly interchangeable principles that serve the purposes of both factions.

Populism swindles popular anger: it is the demagogic co-optation of outrage and revolt.

Consciousness and Emotion

Human consciousness serves as a filter with which to surpass the primitive tumult of the emotions by refining them and reassigning them to that quest for harmony which potentially characterizes human development.

By contrast, giving the upper hand to emotion can blind consciousness and create the kind of obscurity in which the giant squid falls upon its prey. Such is the working method of clientelism and notably of populism, the present vogue for which reflects the decline of proletarian consciousness in favor of a plebeian mind-set. Such is the approach of pundits, demagogues, communications specialists, or rapacious journalists ever in search of the sensationalism that sells papers. Information is reduced to deception, to "scoops," and words are exploited in a systematic way that puts them in the hands of power. Nothing is easier than stupefying and abusing a public about which, once it has been boiled down to statistics, it may be said—after the fashion of despots of every age—that the people are satisfied by bread and circuses.

Religious, ideological, commercial and cronyist propaganda always needs brutes whose faith blindfolds the intelligence of the senses and that of the critical faculties alike. The totalitarianism of money goes beyond brainwashing by instituting the absolute reign of mindlessness.

The adulation of mediocrity and insignificance has always been a feature of authoritarian power. Its modalities, however, differ considerably. Tyrannies of old exalted divine splendor and royal pomp to show the "inferior" classes in what subjection they deserved to be held. Our corrupt democracies do the opposite: the stupidity of the most recent heads of state and their entourages is presented as a model for supposedly imbecilic voters. Mediocrity has become the best of bedfellows for resentment. There is no greater threat to genuine human feeling than disgruntled servility, for slaves invariably ape their masters by oppressing those even weaker than themselves. Think of those idled workers, targets of opprobrium, who spew racism and xenophobia without the slightest awareness of how the multinationals, solely responsible for their plight, must rejoice to see such a fortunate redirection of enmity.

The Intellectual Bloodstain

"All the water in the sea could not wash away an intellectual bloodstain." With the passage of time, Lautréamont's statement has taken on a more and more precise meaning. Hölderlin, who longed for man's self-reconciliation, had already taken a defiant attitude toward intellectuals: "From the bottom of my heart I despise the horde of nobles and priests / But even more the intelligence that commits itself to them."

How are we to account for the tendency of so many artists, writers and thinkers to tolerate, serve, and even celebrate those whom Maurice Blanchard branded for all time with the mark of infamy: "Oh leaders of the people, you piles of filth / infecting our minds and hearts"?

I put it down to the existential rift created by the primacy of intellectual over manual, mind over matter, heaven over earth. Sooner or later we shall have to correct the duality that labor and its fragmentation have introduced into mankind like a wedge splitting a log.

The reconciliation of man and nature heralds the reconciliation of head and body, the restoring of their original unity. The rise of a market civilization has precipitated the decline of man as a human being. The decline of the old world is now signaling the rebirth of a human being freed from the carapace of abstract man.

There is a prejudice that I would dearly like to see swept away once and for all, one that has only too gravely contaminated general opinion: it is time to stop identifying intellectuals with cultured, learned individuals, with scholars, thinkers, poets and discoverers of ideas.

The intellectual is simply someone who sets greater store by the intelligence of the head than by the sensory intelligence of the body as a whole. We are all, to varying degrees, part manual and part intellectual, for centuries of training has taught us to bow to the predatory spirit that the gods were thought to have instilled in us. This split, however, is about to be abolished by a new alliance between mankind and human development. We are destined to surpass the division between head and body.

Though torn away from life, thought aspires to rule it. Originally draped in the vestments of religion, it has been dressed by modernity in the profane garments of philosophy and ideology.

The chasm between ideas and the life instinct shows how the human being has been denatured. It is the cause of the existential malaise that has held mankind in its grip for millennia and that a diagnosis as universal as it is idiotic describes as "ontological."

There is no truth in the claim that human beings are born physically disabled, as if some curse had afflicted them with a genetic defect. On the contrary, humanity's unity was sundered by an unfortunate economic orientation which separated it from itself. The exploitation of man by man obstructed the gradual transcendence of animality initiated in the Paleolithic age—a period characterized by the absence of war and the importance of women. The civilization that followed blocked humanity's evolution toward human fulfillment, sidetracking its progression to a destiny commensurate with its creative potential and reducing it a wretched struggle for subsistence.

Human development was thus arrested at the fetal stage. Market civilization deprived human beings of a normal birth and turned them into pathetic, grotesque runts.

The predatory instinct that typifies the animal kingdom has been transcended in us, made spiritual, even angelic, on the grounds that the "beast in man" must be domesticated. But why did it need to be tamed, if not to shackle it to labor?

How have we failed to understand that the processes of repression and release, as set in motion by the transformation of life forces into labor power, led only to the triumph of a barbarity, which from the Neolithic period until now has turned history into a long trail of blood and guts?

Thought torn away from life drags shreds of that life in its wake which continue to nourish it. Existential suffering has no other origin.

Animality awkwardly straddled by the celestial has made us into hybrids. Consider the way the theater of the world, on its universal stage, presents the pathetic buffoonery of poor wretches born of the unnatural coupling of angel and beast!

Only an art of life—a *dolce stil nuovo*—can rid us of a spirit whose self-assurance can make fake stars glitter amid the mire.

Intellectuals secrete ideology like a spider the thread with which its spins its web. They are captive to what feeds them. They will set themselves free only once they become aware of the cries and murmurs of the body and become the spokespersons of the life within them.

Ideology: An Illness of Being

The best ideas are ever at risk of becoming the worst. In my book *Rien n'est sacré, tout peut se dire* (Nothing Is Sacred— Everything May Be Said, 2003), I defended a principle to which I am still firmly attached: "Tolerance for all ideas, no matter how hateful, how ridiculous or absurd! Intolerance for every inhuman act, be it committed by a state, an ethnic group, or an individual!" The punishment and penal condemnation of racist, sexist, xenophobic, perverse or odious speech is never an adequate response to the need for such sentiments to be eradicated. Incarcerating or applying legal sanctions to the propagators of nauseating ideas is too closely akin to the kind of "populist justice" that is always eager to exorcise the slightest trace of transgression after the fashion of a mob baying for a murderer to be lynched.

At the same time, however, allowing vile ideas to be expressed in the name of freedom of speech by no means implies that they should not be contested. We have seen the most self-evident principles of individual and collective freedom used to justify an ideology that confers its ecumenical blessing on any opinion at all. Basing itself on the intolerable sort of attitude that accuses any opposition to the Israeli government of antisemitism or calls the refusal to approve the oppression of Moslem women racism, an ignorant notion of fairness gives identical weight to the most generous ideas and their complete opposite. To counterbalance praise for women, for nature, or for humanity, the spectacle must of course give a say to champions of misogyny, environmental pollution, xenophobia, homophobia, and—why not, since its stage management is continually in need of upping a notch?—child abuse, rape, and murder.

Not so long ago it was quite acceptable to ape the lame, the hunchbacked or the otherwise handicapped, to mock and shame cuckolds and ravaged virgins. More progressive manners tend to render such attitudes archaic. Today the mental petomania that once raised contemptuous laughter can seem aberrant or grotesque. Are we going to allow the lucrative dramatization of our possible regressions to reinforce the oppression to which it subjects those who seek to live like human beings?

Just as the fanatical proponents of an ever-swelling birth rate condemn millions of children and mothers to death in the name of respect for life, freedom of speech serves as pretext for the scorning and threatening of the freedom to live.

How easily we allow ourselves to be reduced to an abstraction!

It is impossible to exaggerate the noxious impact of thought detached from life. If ideologies continue, even stripped of all religious, political or philosophical meaning, to exercise their destructive power, it is because they are symptomatic of a process of denaturation. They worsen the scission and discord between human beings and loosen the links to the earth that are nevertheless innate. This is the way ideology unbalances and cripples us.

By imposing forced labor the advent of hierarchical societies internalized the gulf between mental and manual. The mind's dominion over the body was thus established, echoing the economy's power over nature and the master's over the slave.

The mind-body antagonism is the same as the antagonism that arises between a collectivity prey to the chaos of its feelings and a leader, temporal or spiritual, who instates a tyranny based on the supposed need to restore order.

The rationality that rules over the instincts strives to repress them. It constrains them, fattens them and unleashes them to the benefit of a dictatorship which spurs conflicts so that it can arrogate the right to resolve them.

The predisposition to misery and self-destruction that allegedly causes humans to remain on all fours and blights their aspiration to happiness is actually the product of a totalitarian system of exploitation under which outbreaks of violence are safety valves for repressed emotions. This is the perpetual motion that abases mankind only to have it rise up against its own humanity.

William Blake denounced the infamous power of intellectualism in exemplary fashion: "In ev'ry infant's cry of fear . . . The mind-forg'd manacles I hear."

The child is the life, the nature and the soil that engenders the human being—the living force that struggles to defeat the haughty and arid abstraction by which lived reality is trapped and gobbled up.

The Man of *Ressentiment*: The Revenge of the Body Frustrated in Its Desires

Whether it avails itself of fascism, of religious fundamentalism, of Bolshevism, of democratic clientelism, or of supposedly revolutionary radicalism, populism is always prompt to attach a yellow star to those whom Céline stigmatized as *agités du bocal* (pseudos) or *têtes d'ampoule* (eggheads). A long lineage, from the Christian apologist Tertullian to the Francoist general Millán Astray, connects those whose cry is "Down with intelligence! Long live death!" An even longer tradition rejoins it surreptitiously, that of all those for whom the intelligence of the head takes precedence over that of the heart.

What is it that makes intellectual faculties so insufferable? The answer is their perpetuation of the supremacy of mind over flesh. The intellect prevents the body from expressing itself, save perhaps from that deep dungeon where slaves curse their jailor.

A sensitive intelligence is supplanted by an abstract one that diverts, corrupts and negates it. The antennae of life, which affect us by means of a kind of resonance, are short-circuited, so to speak, by a process of intellection that captures the song of the earth and transforms it into a celestial canticle.

The fleshly harp that vibrates at the slightest breath of air and causes the whole universe to vibrate in its turn is not completely drowned out by the thundering symphony of commercial rationality, but who notices it?

All the same, an incessant conflict pits the human being against the abstraction of man that in trying to angelize the beast succeeds only in ensuring the triumph of a spiritualized bestiality.

The cunning of the mind consists in concealing the possibility of restoring the unity of the individual. It prevents the development, from childhood on, of a sensitive awareness of the body, of that universal knowledge, at once practical and theoretical, which Rabelais and Montaigne championed and which has inspired a good number of libertarian pedagogues.

The notion of the total man, which has haunted the wildest dreams of humanism, is quite simply *being* becoming conscious of its human destiny.

When it becomes arrogant, intelligence opens the door to stupidity. There was a time when, as overweening as it was, such intelligence had *style*: it still bore the stamp of the vivacity without which ideas are graveyards. But a century prey to no lack of disasters saw the rise of an intelligence that believed itself elevated by the celebration of idiocy merely because its exponents, bards of vacuity, attracted the spotlight. In wastelands devoid of creative imagination, there were those who labored to reanimate the most sordid values of the past—national, religious, ethnic and communitarian identities along with their doctrines of purity and sacrifice—as a counter to the ideologues of antiracism or of the struggle against antisemitism who exemplified an authoritarian and pettifogging humanism which manipulated virtue with a hypocrisy that persuaded their ignominious opponents that it was they who "spoke the truth."

A hidden harmony thus reigned between the inanity of progressive ideas and the redundancy of conservative ones. With striking unanimity all these blinkered people proclaiming their clairvoyance had eventually plunged into the same cesspool.

We behave like intellectuals every time we fall under the sway of the separation of our ideas from our life instinct; every time an abstract idea benefits from the disembodiment and impoverishment of our only unalienable wealth, namely that bodily life to which we generally deny a voice, that physiological, psychological, mental substance to which we do not deign to listen so long as it does not speak to us of anxiety or illness, that mare which we merely infuriate by trying to break her in rather than tame her with gentleness, that life which we strive so hard to stuff so full that it eventually spews out the insult that is death.

Ignorant or erudite, the intellectual in his existential despair is nothing more than a being torn apart whose thought bleeds because it has been severed from life.

Populist demagoguery is a truly sick joke: drawing on the abstraction of culture as an alienated form of life and knowledge, all it can stir up against our extraordinary heritage of art and thought is a rabble of the ignorant, the mediocre and the envious who execrate what they do not want to understand. And this to exalt what? Not the will to live but the will to power which is its degenerate form. Not the poet drunk on life but the compulsive whose mind is possessed by bestial rage.

It may be that in the future, here and there, a few traces may still linger of the nationalism which by virtue of its breadth was the first ideology to replace religion and the myth of a social cohesion governed by a unitary belief. In the days of territorial conquest and capitalist imperialism the "little man" whose portrait was sketched by Wilhelm Reich found in nationalism a trough at which he could feed his pride in a gluttonous frenzy. Today the decadence of states and the decrepitude of their rulers have left him nothing but a balloon that only his *ressentiment* can inflate.

All the same it is neither artillery, nor bombs, nor the rhetoric of racism, xenophobia and fanaticism that bring the high tide of barbarism, but rather the hate, fear and resentment of those whom market civilization robs every day of life and of the self-love without which love of others is doomed to wither.

In the past a chronic warfare set religion and philosophy at odds. That conflict continues in the antagonism between the progressive spirit and conservative obscurantism. But the main clash of arms occurs not in the public sphere, where power struggles have full rein, but instead in the place where it originates, in the inextricable entanglement of the head—*caput*, the chief—and the serviceable body.

So long as we have not overcome the body-mind division we shall remain in a pincer grip between abstract intelligence and the brutality of the survival instinct, between the tainted knowledge to which the masters enthusiastically subscribe and the alleged ignorance of slaves so much vaunted by the proponents of voluntary servitude. So long as a new alliance between the body and its sensory intelligence has not restored our lost unity, our existential misery will endure. No matter how comfortable one's circumstances, the dire threat of regression to the inhuman always lays in wait. There will be no peace in the world without this fundamental pacification.

The victory of the heart does not mean loving some and hating others; nor does it imply the promotion of a disembodied principle of fraternity destined for the garbage heap of humanitarian lies. Only the silent strength of individuals becoming aware of the universal life force to which they contribute can manage to banish inhumanity from the world, for there is simply no place for it in the osmosis now underway between individual and self, between individuals and their peers, and between individuals and the animal, vegetable and mineral realms.

The mutation of man into a human being depends on the daily practice of identifying oneself with the will to live. Not on some mystical illumination but on pleasures enjoyed as so many gifts to a life which offers itself to us and to which we want everyone to accede.

The intellect's sway over the body and its supervision of manual labor is a universal bane. Acting in the name of moral principles, whether heavenly or earthbound, it binds humans to a survival worthy only of beasts.

Its pretension infects the mercenary, the fundamentalist, the demagogue and the rapist as much as it rages within the sophisticated artist, the moralist, or the littérateur.

But, you might ask, are not Montaigne, Diderot, Kierkegaard or Nietzsche intellectuals? Yes, certainly—but they are more embarrassed about it, more eager to extract themselves from it, than a Valéry, a Céline, a Sartre, a Mao, or a Goebbels.

Is the Nazi doctrine, with its promotion of the predatory brute, not the epitome of a speculative stew cooked up by the pointy-headed? Are those who talk of drawing their revolver whenever they hear the word "culture" not themselves cultured? Are they not of the same ilk as the self-appointed *conducătorii* of the people who claim a left-wing pedigree? They hate and love each other, like Hitler and Stalin, because they administer the same Mandate of Heaven. They are the blind followers of the spirit of domination, that spirit which tames matter and guides the lost—having first put out their eyes. Anyone who wields some kind of power behaves like an intellectual; all who use intellectualism as a barricade exhale the rank breath of authority.

While knowledge is certainly not enough to ensure the victory of life, ignorance invariably serves tyranny. Religious and ideological obscurantisms amply demonstrate this by censoring and burning books. Furthermore, the defenses raised by the standard-bearers of an emasculated culture against those who scorn it are a quite inadequate response to the barbarity of the populists and corrupt business class.

Social stagnation and psychological paralysis encourage us to look toward a past whose ruins only weigh us down and to construct a present from a hodgepodge of ideological and religious doctrines all of which have fully demonstrated blood-drenched excess and irremediable failure. Within the fake conflicts where change only perpetuates the unchanging, frontiers are eradicated between enemies that a shared contempt for the life forces unites even as it feigns to set them at loggerheads.

Whatever is not surpassed rots. Happiness sacrificed seeks salvation in damnation and self-denial. Life stripped of its joys finds ready satisfaction in horror. Wounded sensitivity is the anvil upon which torturers are forged. Those who are disabused and defeated by a life whose failure they have themselves orchestrated are the most eager to glorify death.

Wherever the freedom trumpeted is not the freedom to live according to one's desires, beware of those who, in Baudelaire's words, "believe they work for independence by barking in unison." Herd-following individuals do not belong to themselves but rather to the pitiful yet formidable fellowship of hate—hate for oneself and for others. The herd is a reservoir of barbarity, a single drop of which can make it overflow.

We are burdened by living beings who fear and despise life. Their own worst enemies, they see foes in the mirror of their own obsessions. What confusion surrounds us, however. Take someone whose statements veer into racism and xenophobia but who turns out to have a kindhearted nature and a quite unexpected sense of human solidarity; or another person, a supposedly revolutionary spirit who preaches liberation but startles you with odious behavior that bodes nothing good for their professed intentions.

What is the good of ideas that are contradicted by actual experience? For my part I make common cause only with people who help me to make life—mine and that of others—more life-syntonic.

Even though, since time immemorial, we have been confronted by an endless stream of wars and conflicts, we continue to blind ourselves by means of two illusions, namely bleeding-heart pacifism, which is always powerless, and the notion that predatory warfare is graven in our genetic heritage—as if that so-called heritage were not in fact the chance outcome of our distorted evolution.

There is a need to hate ever in search of gratification. Family strife and Hatfield-and-McCoy vendettas are cut from the same filthy cloth as the conflicts that set religious communities, political factions and tribal groups at one another's throats.

Would those filled with *ressentiment* find the Other intolerable if they did not feel they were looking into a murky mirror at the image they have formed of themselves? They need a manufactured figure of evil with which to exorcise their own demons. For them the main thing is neither fear of the intrusive menace of the stranger nor confirmation of that stranger's harmfulness. Instead, they want things to be thus so that the anathema they call down on the Other might rid them of their own insignificance.

They would drown in the tears shed over themselves if only they did not have hatred of the Other as a lifebelt. No dialogue with them is possible: what good would it do to explain that self-hate is part of the long agony that is survival: economized life clamped ever more tightly to compulsive emotions and the release of clogged-up passion?

There is no path out of *ressentiment* other than a commitment to life sparked everywhere. A kind of resuscitation, so to speak, of the life principle which in the heart of the robotic brute has occasionally contrived not to perish.

Which said, that life must re-emerge as an irresistible force, a guarantee of invincibility. Not as compassion but with all the violence of the desire to live, a violence utterly divorced from the violence of the predator.

The life instinct may bend at times, but it never breaks. A time always comes when it stands up straight.

The Last Struggle: An Endemic War between the Party of Death and Commitment to Life

How often we have seen a people hasten toward its own destruction after the fashion of the collective suicide of lemmings. One has only to think of soldiers proudly marching off to war in 1914; of the masochistic hecatomb of the Chinese Cultural Revolution; or of nations glorifying the Ubuesque program of the Nazis and cheering on the crimes of Stalin, Mao, Pol Pot, or Milosevic.

In earlier days, however, passions were easily aroused by the drumbeat of nationalism and the banners of military delusion. Suicidal tendencies were readily draped in the shrouds of an imbecilic glory. By contrast, the totalitarianism of money kills without deception or appeal to the emotions: predatory greed replaces arbitrary reason.

But what impassiveness does not cover up some great affective turmoil? Behind the cold-hearted monster of egoistic calculation the creeping chaos of frustration is ever active. The swarming maggots of life unfulfilled complete the dauntless work of voracious market forces

As Ernst Wiechert notes apropos of Nazism, "From the infinite multiplicity of modest lives by no means reconstructed arose a horror that ravaged the earth and the human heart along with it."

The party of death has a morbid attraction for those whom the rule of greed and programmed despair has convinced to give up on life. More than ever before, this sick fascination is sufficient unto itself. The religious or ideological rationales that it still occasionally masquerades behind are really more like cheap adornments than real disguises. Henceforth "pure and purifying" hate will be the sole motive for placing bombs and instigating massacres.

Though seemingly unforeseen, the scourge of suicide, the galvanizing of death worshippers and the proliferation of kamikaze attacks are really just epiphenomena of the everyday inhumanity that thrives on the dung heap of predation, degrades *mores* and spurs regression to a barbarous past. Such is the agonizing and angst-ridden life which populism sustains by palliative means, setting ethnic, religious, ideological, competing or sports-based communities against one another in merciless conflicts that give an illusory meaning to death. To the murderous insanity thrown up by existential suffering, such populism lends the wings of reason and relevance.

Whether individual or collective, all killing is now part of a war waged by the partisans of death against those committed to life. Ethical appeals and humanitarian sermons have not the slightest effect on explosions of hatred. Only the call for happiness, echoed by one and all, can put an end to them.

Wherever love triumphs over hate, life reasserts its absolute sovereignty. Such love flows not from divine grace, nor from good intentions, nor from New Age mysticism. As the passion of lovers demonstrates, it is the route that life's generosity takes, despite all barriers and opposition, never halting, avoiding ambushes and sidestepping or destroying all obstacles in its path.

The most varied and often the most laughable excuses are offered as hasty justifications for mindless violence and barbarity. The exacerbation of inhumanity and the tactic of scapegoating reflect deliberate actions by state, populist and business mafias hungry to maximize the final profit from the organization of chaos.

If I have so often emphasized the reasons for the unleashing of "ordinary" hate—the thought processes of beings who are dissociated from themselves, denatured and turned into their own worst enemies—it is not out of any claim to clairvoyance or any obsessive tendency on my part but simply to evoke an ever-more-apparent development: I have the feeling that our lost unity is being restored, this as a reaction to the horrendous conditions imposed on individuals and societies, fragmenting and privatizing them and stripping them of all solidarity.

Commitment to life is always in play, continually rising from its ashes, ever ready to illuminate us with the light of its flame.

The paradoxical situation that confronts us is, on the one hand, that everyone has a hazy perception of the subterranean roiling of the volcano whose smoking fumaroles signal the imminence of a social eruption, as witness the recent uprisings in the Maghreb. At the same time the spinelessness of what La Boétie called voluntary servitude transforms the masses into swarming larvae kowtowing to every dictatorial measure enforced by the State at the behest of international financial powers. The results include the degradation of education, health care, social services, public transport, postal delivery, pensions; the decline of the main industrial production sectors (steel, textiles, agriculture); the adulteration of foodstuffs; the hijacking of drinking water; the commandeering of alternative and free energy sources; and chemical, nuclear and pharmaceutical pollution.

Such is your legacy from the fatalism, apathy, and resignation of the older generations, from those who precipitated you into this world with no attempt to help you avoid the bastardization of body and consciousness engendered by commodities, money, power and an economic system which, after reducing life to survival, now threatens every life-form on the planet.

A New Con Game: Ecological Neocapitalism

Nothing is ever completely for keeps. You are on the verge of a time when the global environment, gravely damaged by the frenzy for profit, will be re-landscaped. Although this prospect has been easily discernible for decades, it has taken almost thirty years for the herd of bureaucratized thinkers to notice it.

Just yesterday, under the looming threat of nuclear war, the trumpets of the Apocalypse sounded all around the world. This was followed by an ecological catastrophism that, with admirable conviction, warned of another Apocalypse, the latest, namely the desertification of the world.

Now, however, new songs of triumph are intruding upon the whining and wailing: voices raised heavenward in celebration of a neocapitalism resolved to "improve the lot of the people" while actually swindling them yet again. The funeral oration for a finance capital about to implode has caught the attention of wily scavengers computing the revenue to be derived from a "gentle exploitation" of nature.

A new breed of profiteers is slowly emerging from the shadows, driven by a desire to reanimate the economy and purge a source of income dangerously contaminated by the crookery of stock market dealings and the proliferation of virtual money.

Let us not be fooled. A capitalism with ethical pretensions can only cloak the old exploitation of man by man in the garb of the old humanism. What a fine celebration of nature it is to exalt free energy sources to the skies while simultaneously charging users top dollar! What is actually involved here? The answer is a juicy contract founded on greed and guaranteed by nature's bounty rendered profitable.

But what could be more inconsequential than becoming outraged by this, while by the same token an extraordinary opportunity is presented to us: the chance to plunge into the deepening and widening gap between capitalism on the decline and a new guard on the rise and determined to replace it. Surely it behooves us to intervene, so that the forces of life can sweep away the profit economy and arrogate to themselves the right to unquestionable preeminence?

The apathy and voluntary servitude of peoples gives international mafias a free hand to poison foodstuffs, air, water, and earth. Do not imagine that a voluntaristic and ethical humanism could ever suffice to restore the planet to some natural state. The global denaturing of human beings and the world is what has to be contested.

Beneath the cover that the spectacle drapes over everything like a soporific veil, individual creativity is spreading and reviving, laying the groundwork of a radical new society. Each individual is awakening with their own insight within the obscurity to which the dominant system condemns everything that the projectors of media power fail to illuminate.

Whatever is discovered in the future with respect to sustainable and free energy belongs to all and not to the market. Only a self-managed society is capable of perfecting such discoveries and dedicating them to the common good.

What Is Most Lacking Is Awareness of the Self and the World

In the past, when workers got home harried by their job, they at least had time to reflect on their fate, to grouse and rebel. Consumerist forced feeding has now deprived them even of the leisure to belong to themselves. Exercising an allegedly free choice, they have opted for the "freedom" to be slaves to futility and adulteration and—even more destructive—false needs and artificial desires.

But beware of the backlash! Although the media crawled as readily at the feet of corrupt democracies as they had formerly done under the heel of the last dictatorships, revolt has succeeded in spreading by means of telecommunications networks designed essentially to nourish the market of solitude and shared alienation.

Alone in front of a keyboard or a portable phone, individuals have forged links with oppressed people declaring their refusal of all servitude. They have then proceeded to join them in the street or other public spaces. Along their meandering route, where only a culture of isolation had been circulating, the freedom of one and all has begun to stir. Consciousness may stray but is never completely lost.

It is pleasure in creation that will give birth to a world that we are allowed to enjoy because it occurs to no one to appropriate it. Creation is the perpetual motion of a consciousness arising from the body and continually returning to it. That consciousness, hailing from an obscurity which illuminates it, is the most inalienable part of our passion for life and of the mental force which it produces. It has the power to act within the whirling chaos that is forever carrying us along, and consequently it succeeds at times in favoring those desires that are "dearest to our hearts."

At once matter and energy, this sensitive intelligence guides us into the depths of ourselves, placing us at the heart of a web of resonances where an attempt is made to connect the will to exorcise our demons and the "Brownian" flux where events clash in a world whose tremors we feel.

The adventure begins as soon as we manage to convince ourselves that what we desire deep in our hearts will be granted us sooner or later—on the strict condition, however, that we never think in terms of success or failure. Nothing is more exciting to me than the labyrinthine route down which the *unique* consciousness of our will to live reaches the universal consciousness of the living and brings us to the threshold of a world to be created.

Bidding Farewell to an Inhuman Past

To make things clear enough to be stated with complete confidence, let me return to the veritable witch's cauldron of our present, a place where indeed, swirling up and down, the most horrendous elements of the past stew with extraordinarily powerful potions.

In my opinion, the future will derive its traits from a timeless will to live to which human beings must be grateful for repeatedly raising them up every time wars, massacres, epidemics, droughts or other natural disasters laid them lower than the ground itself.

The collapse of an economy founded essentially on the exploitation of the earth and of human beings is underway, awakening and stimulating an irrepressible force innate in our bodies and indeed present in all that is alive.

What lives within and around us can lay the foundations of a human society by getting beyond mere resistance to oppression, beyond the raging protest in which human creativity has stagnated for too long.

Enabling the birth of a civilization emerging with great difficulty from a devastated world is hardly a relaxing task. And creating the conditions capable of preventing any backsliding calls for continual vigilance.

The best way to explain what I mean by backsliding is perhaps to recall the situation with which my generation grappled.

Far be it from me to say how fortunate you are to have escaped an agonizing past. I am concerned only to warn you against possible aftershocks that might cause a wave of despair to rise suddenly from your doubts and in response to the immensity of the task of reconstructing a world.

How often history has capitulated to acts of collective folly whereby civil behavior has turned briskly into savagery! Just think of the German democracy of the 1930s plunging into Nazi horror.

May you learn how to nip in the bud any attempt whatsoever to restore any form of inhumanity.

Consciousness of the living forces may slumber, but it is never extinguished. The occupations movement in May 1968 sowed radical seeds everywhere that make the world's spring inevitable no matter how brutal the coming winters may be.

Since 1968, patriarchy has come to an end in the sense of a system in which the father's authority over his wife and children served as a model for the power wielded by the State and by the hierarchy of masters running down the social ladder from the highest to the lowest rungs. Even regimes still dominated by agrarian attitudes, such as those of the Maghreb, have recently been threatened with destruction by the renewed spirit of the French Revolution.

You will no longer have to experience the odious ascendancy of the army or the sinister compulsory military where one was taught murder, rape, hatred, contempt and xenophobia. Even if the police continue to fulfill the repressive function assigned them by the State, you will be less at risk of having a cop break your door down with a rifle butt at four in the morning.

After so many years of ruling, torturing and massacring to the cry of "Love one another," Christianity is now nothing but a shred of almost forgotten folklore. The democracy of the supermarket shelves the Bible cheek by jowl with sex toys. Islam, the vogue for which has been mistaken for a religious revival, is destined for the same fate. By contesting an Islamism which acts as a front for business mafias, democratizing Islamic movements will eventually be absorbed by the great blotter of social struggle that the totalitarianism of financial power creates everywhere.

You will no longer have to endure the insufferable scorn directed at women, children and nature on behalf of predatory males. In the 1950s a wife beaten and humiliated by her master and the child mistreated and often raped were more likely to arouse off-color humor than indignation.

It took centuries to get rid of a death penalty whereby a hypocritical society exorcised its endemic guilt. Justice must now take a further step, ending incarceration and banning the ignominy of prison forever.

The glorification of work is now part of the cynical masquerading of the bankers and their civil-servant flunkies. Even as it accuses strikers and retirees of parasitism, a genuinely parasitic capitalism closes their factories and gambles with their assets on the stock market. It reduces useful work in prime sectors of the economy such as steel, textiles, education, health, transportation, or postal services, in favor of work whose sole justification is a salary—and one earned only to be splurged immediately on consumer goods.

You will escape the ideological conflicts that fueled the passions of earlier generations, all the arguments over abstract words, thanks to which (as in bygone days the interpretation of biblical texts or the glossing of abstruse dogmas) Marxism, Leninism, fascism, Freudianism and deviations of every kind taxed the brains of faction leaders and caused the gutters to run with the blood of militants.

I have always had reservations about militantism. I do not question the effectiveness of a "mobilization" of consciences. I readily acknowledge that many a prejudice or injustice has retreated in the face of great movements of outrage and valiant affrays with the oppressor. But the militant's behavior is perverse at its core: how could a true solidarity between the happiness of each and the happiness of all ever be founded upon self-sacrifice and self-denial?

What is given can never be reduced to economic terms. The pertinence and determination of an individual attitude are of a quite different nature. A surge of life will suddenly precipitate the refusal of something intolerable: for David Thoreau it was the State's oppression; for Rosa Parks it was segregation. Militants then take over, serving as spokespersons, but whereas the insurgent creates a zone of turbulence and resonance, shaking up apathy, awakening consciences and breaking down the walls of resignation, the militant sacrifices creative joy to agitprop. The very meaning of emancipation is lost when it is changed into a duty or a moral obligation.

Disentangling the Thread of Life from the Past That Has Hidden It

No matter how strewn with wreckage our inhuman past may be, it never fails to reveal glistening gems in the shape of the great works that genuinely human genius has bequeathed so as to arouse in us the wish to perfect or at least develop them. From now on everyone is at liberty to delve into the libraries and conservatories of universal culture in search of ways to enrich their daily existence and the surroundings in which it is ensconced. Every individual manages his or her destiny alone as they face a brutal point-blank ultimatum: comply with the demands of an arduous survival or examine your desires and fulfill them for the sake of your own happiness and the happiness of others.

It is from our physiological and emotional body that everything which happens to us arises; not that circumstances independent of our will cannot affect us, but just as the smell of fear can excite the predator, we call forth from within us many an occurrence that later seems to us to have been determined from without.

Chance, said Nietzsche, is yourself reaching yourself. The creativity of the human being enjoys an extraordinary privilege: the consciousness of what happens inside us, the light cast on the physiological and psychological magma, on the emotional chaos that either destroys us or builds us up, depending on whether we abandon it to bestiality or dedicate it to the endless largesse of life.

There are more and more of us who have become aware not just that the world we inhabit is also within us but also, and above all, that the individual's resolve to prioritize life over survival has the poetic power to jam up the works of the old world and set the new in motion.

Today nobody is unaware to what extent a predatory economy has for millennia mechanized the life forces and ruled our behavior. Using the pretext of the domination of nature, man has enslaved himself to a system that has brutally impeded his human development.

The resolution no longer to be master or slave and to live free in accordance with desires emancipated from their simulacra means forever eradicating the following:

- The predatory instinct that has its roots in animal nature and is the clearest manifestation of the denaturing of man.
- The dominance of the strongest and the most cunning, as imposed by the cult of competition.
- That guilt which can only be exorcised by blaming others, and which is intrinsic to commercial exchange (since everyone is considered guilty of never sufficiently converting their life force into labor force).
- The sacrifice attendant upon struggles for survival in which the one sacrificed is ever ready to seize the knife of the one doing the sacrificing. Only by seeking their own happiness do individuals come to realize that the happiness of one is inseparable from the happiness of all.
- Tactical, strategic and statistical manipulation of the dictatorship of quantity over quality. The fact is that life offers itself without calculation and expects nothing in return. Life is pure generosity: it counts on nothing and counts nothing.
- The power over others that individuals arrogate to themselves. We do not have to give or receive orders. We do not have to tolerate threats, rebuke or fear.

- The sovereignty of money, which is indispensable to survival and hence one of the chief humiliations inflicted on human beings. So far from contributing to an intense, love-filled and joyous life, money's cold hand does nothing but corrupt it.
- Thought separated from life, source of the abstract system known as ideology which—after the fashion of religion subordinating humans and the earth to the decisions of extraterrestrial and fantastical gods—invents a heaven of ideas, or Spirit, that dictates to a body whose consciousness is ignored and scorned.
- The vicious circles of taboo and transgression, authority and permissiveness, repression and release—contradictions which, instead of being surpassed, are held captive and exacerbated, generating conflicts for which life always pays the price.
- The doctrine of man's inherent weakness as propagated by religions and ideologies that would lose their advantage and dominion if they were unable to mass-produce the cripples to whom they sell crutches.

Love of Life Needs No Ethic

Take care not to mistake the above observations for prescriptions. It is not a question of complying with moral imperatives. The drawback with any ethical injunction is that it is not always in harmony with our desires; that our pleasure sometimes overrides it; that the vitality of our passions finds it austere, even puritanical. The struggle we wage at every instant to make our daily existence happier must be the surest and most relevant basis of our demands.

Making it a duty to reject power, arrogance, pride and presumption still boils down to submission to an abstract voluntarism. Away with the tyranny of good intentions! Rebuke partakes of the despotism that the mind inflicts upon the body. No freedom can be forged in shackles.

Survival knows no rights unaccompanied by duties. Life is a right that no duty must pay for.

The body is our raw material—the *materia prima* in the alchemists' sense. Everything flows from the body, beginning with the human consciousness that refines our instinctual animal nature and transcends rather than tries to throttle it.

Consciousness is humble; the mind is prideful. The one exalts the riches of the body; the other dilapidates them. Thought cut off from life is the embryo of all despotism.

Experience teaches that the life force dissipates as soon as it shows off, attitudinizes and morphs into a will to power. Vitality is an energy which undergoes continual renewal so long as it remains an inner force acting in the arcana of that alchemy whereby we subject our drives, our emotions, our desires and our thoughts to a subtle process of refinement and transmutation.

No sooner is that force imprudently externalized than the alchemical vessel—the *athanor*—cracks. It is owing to a fissure in being that vitality leaks out and flows into the maw of appearances and is devoured. There is no better explanation of why the will to power is vitality stricken by impotence, by an inability to live.

The utility of ethics is distinctly ephemeral. It resembles those laws which to a certain degree guarantee the freedoms of action, expression, thought and individual desire but do no more, ever so briefly, than make the stifling atmosphere in our prisons breathable. Ethics partakes of the kind of justice that governs social relations in the manner of commercial exchange, where equity consists in not doing "too much" harm.

Calls to boycott a product, a policy, or a practice smack of hypocrisy and arrogance if they fail to offer an alternative, one more compatible with the enjoyment of life. Would it make any sense to urge someone who needs the crutches of religion simply to toss them aside?

How can we advocate a boycott of consumption without simultaneously proposing a form of individual and social life that can advantageously replace it?

To reject capitalism and in doing so forgo all the benefits and advantages it has lavished on mere survival would only perpetuate the self-sacrifice that the reign of labor passes off as a virtue. The advances made in capital's factories and laboratories belong to us—not because they were bought with the blood of countless generations but because we want a world where satisfaction is not paid for in any coin or by relinquishing anything at all. Only the attraction and the reality of a richer life can drive us forward by disarming and banishing the inhumanity of the past.

Transcendence of Survival Implies the Birth of a New Kind of Life

Conventional wisdom has long identified the authoritarian presumption of our masters with life-affirming exuberance—as though the baying of the leaders of a pack of hounds could be taken for *joie de vivre*. Compelled for centuries to reason in terms of power and subordination, victory and defeat, and success and failure, the function of thought has been so thoroughly captured by the function of government that the crumbling of patriarchal despotism and the disintegration of the pyramids of hierarchy have visited a powerful backlash upon it.

As a mercantile civilization ruled by power and profit approaches a stage at which even its violence is mitigated, those who claim that the status of intellectuals has sunk into the sort of insignificance from which "spectacular unreality" can barely contrive, for all its smoke and mirrors, to elicit more than a spark of curiosity, the briefest of infatuations, from its hosts of rubberneckers.

Pity the intellectuals, reduced as they are to brawling instead of discovering the life that struggles and sours beneath their endlessly patched-up armor.

But what do we care about the decadence of a thought which by abstracting the living forces denatures and dehumanizes man? What I seek, beyond the schism that fragments man, is an intelligence attuned to the unity of the body and universal life: a thought in search of the human.

All intellectualism is repressive, so it was predictable that it should join the downward trajectory of the old forms of oppression. This was true if only because the decrepitude of a hierarchical system in accordance with which the master ordains and the slave complies was bound to entail the mental and physical castration of both.

Indeed, as repression became more indolent, voluntary lethargy and servitude tended to render it superfluous. An endemic fear seemed to plunge populations into a leaden apathy permeated by hate and resentment. It was as though the nightmare of the end of the world prevented humans from awakening and recovering their lucidity and their dignity.

Yet we know full well that the end of mercantile civilization is not the end of the world but rather the dawn of a new civilization.

There have been decades in which, instead of tilting at the already tottering windmills of capitalism, it would have been better to lay the groundwork of a living society founded on solidarity and destined to replace the old system.

Nor were opportunities to do so few and far between:

(a) The fact that the ferocity of repression was languishing just as much as insurrectional violence paradoxically opened the door to life, which can overcome all opposition thanks to the flexibility of its indomitable persistence.

(b) If mankind seeks reconciliation with nature, from which it emerged but which it has betrayed, let it learn to transform the violence of the death wish into a violence that flows from the will to live.

(c) Let man strive to harness nature's inexhaustible energy to the equally inexhaustible largesse of the life that creates and recreates itself in such profusion.

(d) The wheeler-dealers of short-term profit have flooded consumer society with a "hedonism of the last days" whose motto, "Enjoy today because tomorrow will be worse," is doubly lucrative for them: it helps sales while tightening the shackles of resignation, passivity and fatalism. It is up to us to free authentically experienced pleasure from the gangue that imprisons, falsifies, inflates and commodifies it. The day must come when "being" emancipates itself from "having."

The worst result of the bankers' crimes and the cynicism of the market are less the lies and dishonesty than the occult fascination of money, as though it were the supreme value— the value with the power to buy all others. People who persist in voting for the flacks of big business have the souls of petty chiselers who dream of becoming big-time crooks with impunity. Everywhere the cult of having and predation destroys the human being.

Life is pure gratuity: it offers itself and asks nothing in return. Not only is it incompatible with the economy, which reduces it to lugubrious survival, but it is also capable of liberating us from it.

We have to start over from scratch. Too many would-be revolutionaries have believed they were delivering mortal blows to a capitalism collapsing under the weight of its own absurdity when in reality their blows were nothing but the allegorical haymakers of braggarts. The revolution of everyday life does not consist in freeing the repressed, setting fire to the symbols of oppression, or wreaking vengeance on the puppets of power—on bosses, police, or servants of the State. The old world is quite used to managing the safety valves that violence unleashed can provide for frustrations built up day after day.

For far too long dissenters have been content to start fires in a house whose roof is already in flames. How long it has taken for people to realize that they had best leave their dwelling and try to build another, where the fires of joy will warm their hearts without consuming them!

Once civil disobedience arises less from voluntarism than from the life instinct, no oppression will be powerful enough to resist the surge of freedoms that living calls forth in irresistible waves.

Enhanced by human consciousness, life is a weapon that creates instead of killing. It is the source of a lesson that in these troubled times needs to be heard: what must be contested is the totalitarian system which oppresses us and not the people who believe they are in charge of it when in fact they are no more than its pale avatars.

Too often we have complacently conflated lived experience with the symbols that claim to represent it. With frightening ease we fail to distinguish between analogy and symbol. Their meanings, however, are radically different.

Analogy signifies beings and things viewed via the interplay of their similarities. It is the science of resonances, of those correspondences whose microcosmic and macrocosmic effects have barely begun to be studied.

Symbols serve detached thought. They are analogies manipulated by the mind. They therefore display all the mind's cruelty.

What credit can be given to someone who burns down a bank, murders a boss, or loots a store on the grounds that their act threatens the banking system, ends exploitation, or abolishes the commodity?

"To kill a man is not to defend a doctrine," noted Sebastian Castellio. "It is to kill a man."

So many aggressions and assassinations visited upon poor people unlucky enough to incarnate symbolic figures! So many people immolated for letting some label or other be pinned on them!

At least toll systems or machines do not suffer. No one spills blood by sabotaging the armamentarium of control and extortion. Smashing cash registers, ignoring highway charges or gumming up the bureaucratic gear wheels of State and multinational mafias are arguably ways of protecting citizens from crooked taxes and tithes meant to feed the voracious maw of financial malfeasance. One can hardly object to civil disobedience contesting every sort if diktat.

But our war cannot be limited to browsing amid the ruins of market civilization. On the contrary, it must prepare, beyond all war, to create new conditions for life. That is the only way to break the grip of the commodity once and for all.

You Are the Children of an Endless Spring

I have always felt great happiness at the arrival of children, grandchildren and great-grandchildren.

I despise the sanctimonious "pro-life" politics of those who, under the banner "Let them live," promote the mindless, automatic proliferation of tiny defenseless beings thrust out as fodder to a ravenous and pitiless world. Not the least crime of religious, ideological and profit-driven obscurantism is the dooming of millions of children to lovelessness, poverty, illness, delinquency, ferocious predation and economic, military and sexual exploitation.

At the same time I refuse any state or authority the right to impose Malthusian constraints upon us. Everyone is entitled to have children or to choose to have none. It is quite obvious that making the quality of life of the newborn paramount will completely preclude the sort of excessive birthrate that inevitably leads to the cruel elimination of the surplus.

That the infant should be desired, that affection should surround its cradle, that the guarantee of a happy destiny should be its gift of welcome—such, to my mind, are the sole prerequisites to a freely taken decision to reproduce. Surely these demands, moreover, are one of the things that most clearly distinguish the new generations from the old, so long burdened by the tyranny of the family, moral and religious hypocrisy, contempt for women, and the rule of the strongest and most devious?

Provided they are known, recognized and intelligently loved, children and adolescents strive to endow their life with the sovereignty refused it for such a long time by the totalitarianism of the market and its political henchmen. However confused and hesitant their steps, I feel that they are obscurely guided by that human evolution which is the destiny promised to mankind from the beginning.

What would the reasons for my attachment to children be worth if they did not flow from a desire that has always been dear to my heart? Since the pleasures of the flesh are sufficient unto themselves, why have I wanted to burden love's already frail branch with fruit that ripens with every season of life? The stupid fantasy of the perpetuation of one's name has always been foreign to me, and even more so the odious power, so commonly sought, to corrupt malleable and fragile beings.

I am convinced that conceiving a child is at once an act of love and a particular manifestation of the creative genius of two people. That offering the gift of life to a small being might on occasion replace other forms of creation and love is of strictly no consequence, for only by ceaselessly renewing the awe and affection from which the infant draws sustenance can we enable it to find its way to a singular destiny.

I do indeed have the strange feeling that I am intimately "governed" by what remains life's great mystery: the desire to create living matter capable of fertilizing a barren world with its love. At the risk of repeating myself, let me say that I consider creativity to be the true defining trait of human beings, a trait of which they have been deprived by an obligation to work that only plunges them into misery.

When you were born I rediscovered the promises which my childhood had innocently trusted but which, a loving family notwithstanding, the vile and rapacious dominant culture had disparaged and mocked.

I once dreamed of an existence replete with generous feelings in which I would gratify human beings and animals alike. Instead, as the years passed, I sank into a slimy social world where animals were tortured, sometimes in the name of science; where an everyday contempt deemed women inferior to men, even the most stupid of men; where children, viewed for the most part as a nuisance, were accommodated solely by reason of their future profitability; and where humans, proud but resigned, fed themselves into the mill of daily labor only to emerge broken and softened up for the harrying of programmed cretinization. Those were times when arrogant intellectuals stigmatized the allegedly imbecilic masses without realizing that such contempt would backfire and make them the contemptible ones.

How, in such circumstances, could the heart *not* either "break or become as hard as bronze" (to borrow Chamfort's phrase)? A society that brutalizes the sensibilities of children is a criminal enterprise.

Fighting for Life Is Not Fighting against Death

Our actions and thoughts have been incorporated into a perspective in which death is the convergence and vanishing point.

How have so many generations remained so resigned and complaisant as to accept that their existence, their thoughts, their feelings, their actions and their works should have no reference point other than the grave; and that everything comes into being, grows and reproduces under the threat of imminent annihilation, irreversible entombment?

I do not deny the inevitability of death (although the future may reserve surprises in this regard). I merely reject the way the notion of decline and death dominates the course of everyday life, shackling its joys, dissipating its aspirations and clipping the wings of hope. I am repelled by the everyday death that is held up as a supreme guide, the torture, initiated in infancy, that glories in the systematic degradation of human beings, their diversion from the pleasures of living and their sacrifice on the altar of the gods to which their denaturing has given rise. Whatever makes us pay the slightest attention to these absurd and cruel entities that, after the fashion of the Parcae, spin and weave the thread of destinies, the best part of which they then lop off and discard?

Survival is nothing but a long agony that denatures death itself. The fact is that the end of suffering cannot be equated with the end of a life which ought not to be extinguished before its desires have been satisfied and its resources exhausted—before closure can come in the euphoria of complete fulfillment.

We always come to the same conclusion: no sooner was man obliged to transform his life force into labor force than vital energy was confined to a struggle for survival governed by the quest for profit. Quality of life gave way to a quantified existence. "Being" was replaced by "having." The gradual impoverishment of the potential for life favored a time continually flowing away and being lost rather than other kinds of temporality, as for instance the concentrated time of ecstasy, desire, dreaming, imagination, and emotional shock.

We survive in a succession of hours and days characterized only by wear and tear, decline, and the due date of the void: a totalitarian as opposed to a living time, life dribbled away in regrets. Well and truly poor are those who have no wealth but their past.

Does giving priority to real life actually postpone the day of one's death? Those who try it have no interest in the answer to that question.

Live as though you were never going to die, and explain yourself to nobody!

The end of market civilization implies a reversal of perspective: we aim to substitute the perspective of life for the past's perspective of death.

We are the pioneers of a society founded on new alliances between humans and their bodies, humans and the earth, humans and all natural beings, animal, vegetable or mineral. We are reinventing time.

The banning of a number of practices and customs does not go beyond a kind of ethical voluntarism—do-goodism, so to speak—so long as it is not founded on a commitment to what is most alive, most generous and most human in us. Our desires, however varied, are the starting point of any such construction. And they are inseparable from the consciousness that refines them.

Our sole solid foundation is everyday existence: what it is and, inseparably, what we want it to be.

This is the only yardstick that can guide us and prevent ideas such as that of liberty from morphing into abstract notions cut off from living reality. The liberty of man is not my liberty. My freedom is not the freedom of free trade, that of the struggle for survival, or that of the right of the strongest and most devious. The freedom of predation denies my freedom to live according to my desires. The freedom of my desires destroys itself if it is identified with the freedom of the predator.

For a Festive Society

Our carnivals are for the most part no more than mild relief for sorrow-stricken hearts. We were born, however, for a society in which *joie de vivre* routs everything opposed to it.

A festive life should not be confused with the kind of exuberant outbursts that are paid for in the currency of disillusion and misfortune. Such a life is incompatible with joys whose essence is so fragile that even as we grasp them we feel that they must soon fade. It cannot be achieved by way of contemplation, but it is even less accessible via the sort of hedonism which, aware that ennui kills, promotes the belief that it can be tricked by overindulgence in the pleasures of the bottle, the table, or the bed of looming death.

On the contrary, festive life is a continual flux that carries along, fertilizes and gives meaning to everything that motivates us. It calls for a society flooded by the human generosity to which everyone, rich or poor, has aspired at some time. It requires a material abundance founded on the wealth of "being"—a wealth that treats "having" solely in terms of pleasure taken in its banishment.

Sooner or later, atop the ruins of the tyranny of commerce, generalized self-management—no matter what one calls it—must become the groundwork of a genuinely human society, a society from which money has vanished; where one benefits oneself by bringing benefits to others; where individuals enjoy the leisure to give, and to give themselves, without making any sacrifice; where brother- and sisterhood propagate the minor attentions of gracious friendship: "You like this necklace? It's yours then!" Or: "This thing appeals to you? Take it, it's a present."

The citizens' groups that mercantile imperialism tends to spur into being against itself everywhere in the world promote a direct democracy, in opposition to the parliamentary variety, that replaces citizens by actual individuals. The rejection of inhumanity leads to a projected society in which the human-ization of the world and that of the individual cannot be separated.

Let me reiterate that all opinions, no matter how absurd or repugnant, must be allowed free expression. On the other hand, no barbaric acts should be tolerated.

Inhumanity is not open to question or debate: it is to be universally condemned. It invalidates the very notions of majority and minority. If it should happen in an assembly that a barbaric motion is put to the vote, I contend that no majority decision has the authority to support it. I reject the right of the greater number to prescribe a measure whose cruelty is beyond doubt (as, for example, the death penalty).

No majority is entitled to issue decrees harmful to the interests of life. The human choice of a single person carries more weight than an inhuman decision approved by many. The quality of life abrogates the dictatorship of numbers, of the quantitative.

Resolving to "take care of our own business" will constitute a great forward step in the struggle against the corrupt busi-ness system that lays waste to beings and things. It will fall to you to debate the creation of territories at last freed from the grip of the commodity. You will have to institute the rule of gratuity, organize the demise of money, and supervise the temporary use of a currency restricted to the exchange of goods and services, a currency that is non-capitalizable, non-accumulable. . . .

All the same, you must never lose sight of the fact that a self-managed arrangement confined to the economy will tolerate the maintenance of the regime of survival, that rift between human beings and themselves which spawns of all other rifts and hatreds.

We are so accustomed to paying for whatever we receive that the fear of having to settle the bill arms us against the gift. It is not *for nothing* that the economic law of supply and demand shapes the survival of the most diverse of peoples worldwide.

Let us stop scorning our ability to invent a new life. Everything is given, nothing is owed, because we are entitled to give what has been given to us. Such is the basis of human generosity.

As life economized, *survival* is subject to the laws of the commodity. That is why the right to survival necessarily entails duties. *Life*, by contrast, means rights alone, with no quid pro quo. Its sovereignty signals the end of economic tyranny, the abrogation of the principle of "having"—no more outstretched hand expecting value for money.

Surrendering neither to manipulative egoism nor to contemptuous egotism guarantees happiness. My only possible concern is the combined transmutation of the self and the world. I have but one passion, one which embodies all the others: to wish "from the bottom of my heart" for such a change to come about with its infinite ramifications.

The metamorphosis to which I aspire is that of man into human being, for the human being continues to dwell within us awaiting eventual revitalization. Human being is the being that each of us remains and that remains within each of us, no matter how hard we try to reject or ignore it.

The revolution of the human race is, quite simply, the reconciliation of humans with their destiny. It will transcend the agrarian and industrial revolutions which not so long ago inflicted on humanity the injury of a history made by itself against itself. For too long we have wasted our energy struggling in vain against a morbid fate which reduced us to nothing. We are now about to devote our forces to a destiny yet to be constructed whose building blocks are the scattered fragments of an imperishable life.

Contrary to the sickening regurgitation of forms of communitarianism whereby the individual identifies with a religion, a nation, an ethnicity, a tribe, or an ideology, I can only repeat that there is only one valid identity: to be, over and above all, a human being.

We may well be witnessing a combined rebirth of nature and mankind. As though the fury of a land too long brutalized by labor and greed were seeking a gradual pacification by means of a hitherto inconceivable alliance. As though, once liberated from its age-old servitude, the earth were announcing the resurrection of the living, free being that mankind has buried within itself. As though the end of the exploitation of the soil and subsoil, as hitherto decreed by the putative mandate of heaven, certified the marriage of heaven and earth. As though, lastly, the union of human beings with their bodies and with the chthonian components of those bodies broke the chain forged by religion for the benefit of the gods and their blind followers, thus making way for an osmotic relationship, a universal symphony, the ligature of each of whose notes to the work as a whole restored the original meaning of the term *religio*.

The dogma of the intrinsic weakness of man usually seeks justification by adducing the depressions that nobody avoids and that exacerbate morbid imaginings, amplify doubts and instill irrational fears. But are we not all victims of an artificial interpretation of the biological rhythm in which exuberance and melancholy alternate in a sort of systolic-diastolic way? The dominance of the death-oriented perspective dramatizes this natural rhythm to the point of distorting it, pointing up depressive states and downplaying joyful ones, whose transience is exaggerated. The death-centered view is a function of our denatured condition.

Beset myself by surprise onsets of melancholia, I have found consolation by drawing an analogy with the tides. Like waves lost in the ocean of life, are we not subject to ebbs and flows, to alternations between joy and distress, exaltation and dejection, vivacity and lethargy?

We are not governed by lucky or unlucky stars, by some capricious fate, by divine intervention, or even by a nature eager to exact dues for its gifts. We are part of a living sea that advances and recedes, turn and turn about.

Low tide leaves wrack and rubbish on the foreshore that high water then conceals in its hidden depths. Likewise we feel brutally overrun by a mass of sordid thoughts, shameful emotions and unhealthy images which, once the rising tide of life submerges them, cease bothering us, fade, and vanish.

No sooner, however, does the vital tide ebb than unrefined animality insinuates itself into our emotions, startling us. As it passes through, it scatters the remains of unfulfilled or dead passions that bear witness to our denaturing and seems to tarnish past, present and future. The humors that for no apparent reason shake and tumble us are surely nothing but a continual oscillation between forward and backward currents whose movements we should be well advised to join after the fashion of a seasoned swimmer who has the secret of being one with the flow.

Our torments, irrational fears and pathological tendencies are not washed away by the high tide, but rather covered by a vital force that churns and soothes them. Why should we not bank on powerful moments of life to advance a human consciousness well able to take our residual animality in hand, at once embracing and surpassing it? That exercise has nothing unprecedented about it: no true lover has failed to discover the joy of refining the rudimentary genitality of coitus and transforming it into erotic passion.

The best way to avoid ever giving up life's gifts is to desire them incessantly, as though granting them to us reflected a generosity inherent in its nature. That said, such manna still needs to be incorporated into the riches of "being," not into the ledgers of "having."

Every kind of cult consecrates. But life is not a sacred thing. Life is utterly indifferent to ritual, devotion, and mystical or contemplative visions. Vital energy demands nothing at all save deliverance from the exploitation and economy that hobbles it. The alliance between being as it discovers humanity and nature will reveal the inexhaustible power of life.

Nature's generosity delivers everything wholesale. It is up to us to sort the wheat from the chaff and gather the best part of terrestrial largesse.

The secret of endlessly recreated love lies in its fusion with the love of life. To separate the two is to deprive love of its center of gravity.

Let no one weave the web of your destiny in your stead. Be the only one to decide, and this in full awareness that hostile and demobilizing forces are at work within you also. Steer as close to life as possible, and tell yourself, between perils and joys, that life is there, present in you, even in the shadow of death.

Despite doubts as I grope my way forward, the adoption of a few practical principles has helped me navigate a little less blindly through the existential labyrinth where the body and its consciousness join forces in a vital surge to foil what conspires to divide and destroy them. These principles have nothing to do with either a set of magical spells or a book of recipes. The relief they have afforded me can be partaken of solely by virtue of the way they are applied:

- Desire everything; expect nothing.
- Do not measure either yourself or others. No life is subject to calculation.
- Compare yourself to nothing and to no one. Each being is unique. Only "having" uses scales and weighs each individual like a commodity.
- Be the human being that you are becoming.
- Life gives you what you give life.
- Offer yourself; never respond to demands.
- Lived authenticity is unburdened by representation.
- Life qualifies; survival quantifies.
- Intention opens the door to desire.
- What is desired from the bottom of the heart tends to be attained.
- Survival views intelligence only as mere cunning. Life is the triumph of sensitive intelligence. The first must be paid for; the second is given.

Let no one take it into their head to give you orders! Banish from your circle anyone who displays contempt and arrogance. Distrust obedience. If the taming of dogs, wolves and wild animals is supposed to demand a spirit of mastery and impeccable authority, constraining one's peer or complying with orders means regressing to the animal level.

No truly human society will see the light of day without eradicating the power that any man or woman arrogates to themselves from another.

Confronted by fear and a flood of wild feelings, I force myself to go down like Orpheus into the Erebus of my uncontrollable emotions before reascending slowly toward those illuminations of consciousness which, as uncertain and flickering as they may be, do at least *reflect*.

So as not to be obliged to turn to Eurydice with reassurances that I do not feel, I make sure to place her ahead of me, lavishing all the love in the world upon her.

Whatever your preoccupations, may you harmonize your own passions and discover in yourselves that magnetic pole whence the harmony of the whole world springs and radiates. The Great Work of existential alchemy is the transmutation and refinement of every single instant.

Whoever learns to love themselves needs no lessons in loving others. Happiness shared chases away misfortune. Only when it changes into "having" does it provoke hate-filled envy and destroy itself.

What drives people to fight one another so resolutely, under whatever pretext, is misery, and chiefly the misery of beings dispossessed of their own existence. They feel so deprived of life that they never tire of depriving others of it. The commitment to death whereby individuals celebrate their betrothal to nothingness is powerful indeed, yet life is stronger still. Life is the wager we must lay every day.

How else are we to get rid of those crutches which religions and ideologies sell to the handicapped, whom they cripple from birth, than by disseminating the conviction—to the point where it permeates thought, the body, and social mores—that life is not an object to be exploited, that no aspect of it should be commodified, and that it has no place for either guilt or atonement. Life is just life, sown far and wide so that from every seed individuals may bring their humanity to fruition.

Beware of those who contest barbarity without laying the foundations of a society that derives the power to banish it from happiness. How could armed groups ever truly overcome dictatorship when they are themselves imbued with a military spirit?

"Take care that the enemy you are fighting is not already inside you!" Should not this kind of warning encourage us to take aim not at humans, but rather at the system that manipulates them?

The fact that old age and death will one day get the better of me has never convinced me of their inevitability. Market civilization has duped the world and made a category mistake by mechanizing the life forces. Here we stand, confronted by that civilization's last gasps, by the pathetic and risible paradox of a survival more comfortable than ever and a life so lethargic that a *danse macabre* suffices to divert it.

Under the scalpel of science the mechanics of the body is gradually losing its mysteries. Medicine makes progress in the art of galvanizing individual health so as to ensure everyone's productivity in the labor market. The surgeons of the soul are not far behind. All would be fine if only humans were cars whose operation was the province of conscientious and skilled mechanics.

But that is not so. Mechanical reactions are precisely what shatter and denature our life instincts. The prevailing forms of therapy do not grasp and serve to conceal the degree to which we are composed of unexplored universes. Do we have any idea of what dwells within us and provokes anxiety, terror, feelings of well-being and sudden bursts of joy?

Our inner recesses are peopled by monsters that demand nothing so much as to find themselves tamed. What is their origin, if not the attic of our great mansion, where our brain, though designed to discover and fertilize vast territories, has been pared down to the barest minimum, colonized by the spirit of predation, and conditioned to repress natural instincts, animal emotions and the volcanic potential of the senses?

Whether mainstream or alternative, medicine cannot evade an economy that reduces life force to a survival that is a function of work. Only the will to create a destiny for oneself can give voice to the wild outbursts of our frustration, thus assimilating them to the language of humanity with no loss of ardor. Granted, it is no easy task to identify our desires and restore to life those which have been perversely oriented toward death, but such is the passion that revives all others.

Unprecedented questions now arise that challenge past and present conceptions and science. Do our physical organs have consciousness? What about the visceral brain, intercellular communication, the power of autosuggestion, placebos, or a form of time that contradicts the doctrine of time's ineluctable flow? What are our dreams, traversed and fertilized by the imagination, and how do the resonance effect and coherent fields work? To what extent does our existence condense the lineage of the generations from which we descend and to what extent does it enshrine the seeds of the generations to come? By what alchemy does our destiny regulate the transmutation of the desires that closest to our hearts? Of what is the energy of ephemeral and constant desire capable? How is it that I am, at one moment or another, my own enemy?

Answers to these questions can be furnished only by whatever of universal life resides within us.

Rediscovering our kinship with the animal realm means reconciling with the beast in us, refining instead of opposing, repressing and allowing it only cruel forms of release. Our humanization entails granting animals the right to live in accordance with their own specificity.

Killers of men, women and children are a vile brood who must assuredly disappear. And, along with them, all those who massacre animals, trees and landscapes.

The time must come when a great reconciliation takes place with the beasts and even—who knows?—among the beasts themselves. The time of alliance with the body, and with the life which the earth carries just like the woman—its analogical double—whose desire to give birth only purposefully it will eventually echo.

Nothing could be further from my intent than to get the feeling of having done my duty. All constraint is anathema to me. At the same time, I am well aware that my whole being becomes a "duty to be" just as soon as desire arises and takes aim at fulfillment. This process of becoming is what breathes life into me and, thanks to the oneiric condensation of time that desire contrives, causes the future to come to meet me, offer me its happiest emanations and nourish my present with its benevolence.

In diametrical opposition to tragedy—the word is related to the *tragos*, the poor skinned goat—and likewise to comedy, the catharsis of laughter, I go forward alone, surrounded by the countless creatures, present and yet to come, that the great sower of life casts to the four winds and that I gather in a laborious yet passionate manner. Each partakes of the egregore that distils the totality of singular, collective and universal life forces.

May the poetry of life be our ultimate weapon! It captivates without capturing, gives but never commandeers, and propagates an aspiration for happiness that revokes the need to kill.

We are dissatisfied only because we fail to be insatiable.

History is the outcome of a deviation. It has been made by mankind against mankind. It has betrayed man by misdirecting man's natural evolution. It has impeded his transition from animal to human and spread-eagled him between two conditions that incessantly divide his being. It falls to you to liberate humanity from the limbo where it languishes and restore its rightful destiny. That task is less daunting than a facile rhetoric suggests: all that is required is the mustering of the universal movement of all those, ever more numerous, who seek the sovereignty of life.

I have no yearning for immortality save in the form of the timeless and evanescent smile that Lewis Carroll gave the Cheshire Cat. Be ready for it to manifest itself as you make your way at leisure through a world where being has supplanted having.

Le Pays des Collines, October 5, 2011

Afterword

It Is January

by John Holloway

It is January. So important for the children. For us too. And now it is more January than ever.

So much tells us that it is December, the month of closure. That things are going downhill, that humanity is coming to an end, that there is no way out of the capitalist dynamic of death.

But tell that to your children, to their children, to the children of the world. Tell them they have no future. Impossible, of course. That is what is so wonderful about the title of this book. It does not permit us the self-indulgence of December-thinking; it pushes us forcefully into January.

January, the month of Janus, the god with two faces. One looks back, just like Benjamin's angel, the angel of history: "His face is turned toward the past. Where we perceive a chain of events, he sees one single catastrophe which keeps piling wreckage upon wreckage and hurls it in front of his feet." But Benjamin's angel has only one face. It is true that he "would like to stay, awaken the dead, and make whole what has been smashed," but he is unable to, for the "storm irresistibly propels him into the future to which his back is turned, while the pile of debris before him grows skyward. This storm is what we call progress."

Unlike Benjamin's angel, Janus has another face. This one looks forward, to a world of possibility, a world that could be, that is not-yet. The first face holds us trapped in the past, in the ruins of history, in the downward spiral rushing us toward human self-annihilation, but the face that looks forward looks to a world of worlds to be created. Writing to our children and their children, and to ourselves, we must say, as Raoul does, "Let us stop scorning our ability to invent a new life."

The critique of capitalism is shaken, pushed forward to the question of revolution. Closure is unacceptable. We cannot write to our children and say, "Tough, sorry, history is closed now, you've arrived too late, the only way is down."

Now it is more January than ever. Never before has history looked so starkly in both directions at once: toward disaster and toward emancipation. Human self-annihilation is more firmly on the agenda than ever before. Genghis Khan, Napoleon, Hitler could cause enormous destruction and despair, but they did not have the means at their disposal to seriously threaten the survival of humans on the earth. Now, there is a motley host of leaders who can achieve that effect simply by pressing a button and unleashing nuclear war. Now too, it has become clear that the cumulative effects of the way that we live are destroying the physical preconditions of human life, through climate change or contamination and exhaustion of the water supply. Now, at this moment, we are living through an upsurge of hatred against other people, a rise of fascism and racism and sexism that was quite unthinkable twenty years ago. The backward-looking, deadly face of Janus stands out so strongly that the other one fades in comparison.

Wonderful, then, are the opening words of this book: "You are privileged to have been born at a crucial moment in history. A period when everything is being transformed and nothing will ever be the same again. . . . One civilization is collapsing and another is being born. The misfortune of inheriting a planet in ruins is offset by the incomparable joy of witnessing the gradual advent of a society such as history has never known—save in the shape of the mad hope, embraced by thousands of generations, of some day leading a life at last freed from poverty, barbarism and fear. . . . Little by little a new society is emerging from the mist." Here is the other face, the one that opens, the one that looks forward and creates. Here is the face that we must think and act and live.

We must all write letters to our children and the children of the world. The very idea of this book pushes us into a different way of thinking. We can all do it, and indeed it is difficult to come away from this book without thinking, "What would I have to say in this letter?" It cannot be a happy-happy-Disneyland letter. That would be profoundly dishonest. In some way it would have to start from, or at least have as a backdrop, the spiral of destruction in which the world is caught at the moment. But it absolutely cannot be a letter of closure, it has to say, "Go and change it, go and create this new society that is emerging from the mist." But how?

But how? And the answer comes tumbling out of our mouths, from our pens, from our fingers: we do not know / in a million different ways. We have learnt a not-knowing. Perhaps that is one of the important things to be passed on to our children. It used to be that revolutionaries would know the way forward and explain it to the masses, spreading class consciousness, telling them what must be done. That failed, disastrously. And now we know that we do not know. Back to Socrates, at least in the sense of dialogue, but not in the sense of proving ourselves cleverer than our interlocutor. Rather, forward to the Zapatistas and their wonderful "*preguntando caminamos*" (asking, we walk). Our not-knowing does not lead to despair but to a collective discussion of how we go forward. And in the process, we realize that this asking is not a means to an end, that it is the end, an end that begins. In asking for the road forward we are already building the ways forward, creating a different politics, a different world: a world not of monologue but of dialogue, a world of mutual recognition. Instrumental politics reached its maximum expression in Lenin's *What Is to Be Done*, and it was a disaster. Now we must go asking.

But the asking is already more than an asking. It is an asking filled with experience. As we walk asking, we see a well-paved road stretching in front of us with a signpost pointing to Social Change, and at the entrance there are people pointing the way forward and calling, "This way, this way for social change! If you want to change the world and make it a better place, come this way!" And we say, "No, not that way! That is the road of telling, and asking cannot walk the road of telling." Perhaps we do not know how to change the world radically, but we know that it is not through the State. Many have gone that way and have died trying to create a better world through the State, and all have returned either disillusioned or corrupted and cynical. The paths of radical change do not lie through the State, simply because the very existence of the State is so integrated into the reproduction of the capitalist system that it can do nothing other than try to reproduce that system. The road of the State takes us farther into the dynamic of death, destruction, annihilation.

We must make our own paths by walking on them. Or rather: we make our own paths by dancing on them. Perhaps *"preguntando bailamos"* instead of *"preguntando caminamos"*: asking, we dance. We dance our way forward, breaking the rhythms of our doing, breaking the logic, the grammar of everyday life. Because that is the key to revolution: breaking the rhythms, the grammar, the logic, the patterns of the daily process of capitalist reproduction. Or, as Raoul famously puts it in his *Revolution of Everyday Life*, "People who talk about revolution and class struggle without referring explicitly to everyday life, without understanding what is subversive about love and what is positive in the refusal of constraints—such people have a corpse in their mouth."

In the revolutionary tradition, revolutionary activity and everyday life were defined by their separation. The revolutionary militant proves his commitment by sacrificing the comforts of the home, by turning his (typically his) back on family and friends and going off like a priest to dedicate his life to militancy. Radicalness and everydayness seem to be polar opposites. Yet it is just the opposite. A militancy that reproduces the distinction between public and private creates its own superficiality: revolution becomes focused on the transformation of the public realm without touching the separation of public and private that is inherent to the reproduction of capitalism. The paradoxical result is that militancy then leads to a timid, half-hearted concept of radical change. The problem with the revolutions of the twentieth century was not that they were too radical, but that they were too timid, with a bravery trapped in a world of sacrifice and power. They did not go far enough.

The turn to the everyday is no retreat into the private. It is no lowering of expectations. Rather it is just the contrary, it is a dramatic intensification of what we mean by revolution. When Vaneigem says in this book, "So long as we have not overcome the body-mind division we shall remain in a pincer grip between abstract intelligence and the brutality of the survival instinct," this goes far beyond what Lenin or Trotsky or Rosa Luxemburg demanded of revolution. The overcoming of the mind-body divide is a matter of everyday practice, yet it breaks radically with the totality of existing social organization. Marx points us in the same direction when he says, in effect, at the very beginning of *Capital*, that so long as we continue to relate to one another by exchanging our products as commodities, we shall remain in a pincer grip that will take us to the annihilation of humanity. Or Adorno: "So long as we remain trapped within identity, we shall repeat Auschwitz over and over again."

Three lightning flashes in the night that cut through the separation of public and private. Three variations on a theme, for it is clear that the practice-thought of identity is inseparable from the coagulation or fetishization of the flow of social relations inherent in the exchange of commodities, and that the separation of mind and body too is part of the commodification of human relations. Three simple statements that focus on everyday activity and resonate into all the nooks and crannies of human sociality. Three startlingly simple diagnoses of what is wrong with the world, three simple prescriptions for how to stop our collective self-destruction. Three simple rejections of the State, for, by its very existence, the State identifies, the State separates the mind from the body, and the State promotes the commodification of human intercourse. But this is no retreat into the private: it is a call for the construction of an alternative sociality. More, it is the recognition of a new sociality that is already in process, based on the overflowing of identity, the refusal of commodification, the breaking of the separation of mind and body. In a world based on the totalizing of these practices, this means a demoralizing, a breaking away, a dancing in the opposite direction, a creating of cracks in which the world that we want begins to flourish. Back to the opening words of the book: "You are privileged to have been born at a crucial moment in history. A period when everything is being transformed and nothing will ever be the same again. . . . One civilization is collapsing and another is being born." This other world is—or better—these other worlds are being born in the cracks, in the subjunctive crevices of the not-yet. But will they thrive?

Revolutionary poetry. It is a matter of revolutionary poetries and their force, as Raoul told us in *The Revolution of Everyday Life*. Capitalism reproduces itself through the operation of its laws, the laws of capitalist development. Revolutionary poetries are the breaking of those laws, the rupturing of the rhythms of capital, the creating of a different time and space. These are poetries in which all concepts move in-against-and-beyond their identifying limits, their limiting identities, creating literary works of breathtaking beauty: Blake's "Proverbs of Hell," Marx's *Capital*, Adorno's *Negative Dialectics*, Bloch's *Principle of Hope*, Raoul Vaneigem's *Revolution of Everyday Life* and his other works including this book, many of the communiqués of Subcomandante Marcos, and Galeano, to mention just a few. The beauty of these works is significant because it reminds us that these cracks, these subjunctive crevices, for all the practical difficulties that they face, can thrive only if they are places-times of beauty, poles of attraction that draw people into them and out of the drudge of survival. If the cracks become places of self-sacrifice, they are already fading back into the world that surrounds them. "He whose face gives no light, shall never become a star" (Blake, "Proverbs of Hell"): the same can be said of the many, many creations of a different sociality. Revolutionary poetries are not just a matter of words and concepts but are above all practical: they are the often hesitant, always contradictory, sometimes wrongheaded pushes toward a different world, a world worthy of our children and the children of the world-to-come.

Our hopes lie in the cracks in society, but these are cracks also inside us. The self-antagonism of this society reproduces itself inside us as a self-antagonism. The moving in-against-and-beyond capital is a moving in-against-and-beyond ourselves. Our poetry of word, thought, and action must reach in and touch our self-antagonism, reach in and find the opening of January where it seems that there is only the closure of December. Raoul makes a distinction between the proletarian and the plebeian: "The proletariat was conscious of the struggle to be waged against the exploitation of man by man. Plebeians by contrast possess only the animal's survival instinct: their emotional blindness is governed by nothing save the power of the predator and the cunning of the prey." Yes, but the proletarian and the plebeian exist inside all of us, just as the antagonism between life and survival is inside all of us. Revolutionary poetry, of word, thought, and action, is a reaching out to, a trying to touch, the proletarian inside the plebeian, the life hidden under the coat of survival. It is not principally the struggle of one group against the other, the proletarians against the plebeians, but the struggle in all we do to give strength to life in-against-and-beyond survival, to the proletarian in-against-and-beyond the plebeian. In these terrifying times in which the plebeian in Raoul's sense is celebrating its orgies in east and west, it is more important than ever to think not in terms of identities (plebeians of the right against proletarians of the Left), but in terms of flows of anger which swirl between the proletarian and the plebeian: flows of anger of which our revolutionary poetry is an active part.

And now, dear reader, it is your turn. Close the book or, better, leave it open, pick up your pens, and write a letter to the children of the world to come. When I received the invitation to write this Afterword to Raoul Vaneigem's book, I jumped up and down for joy: it is an honor beyond imagination. And now it is for you to continue. And you will see that to write for the children born and unborn is a different exercise, one that inevitably takes us into January.

June 4, 2017, Puebla

My thanks to Edith González Cruz, Panagiotis Doulos, Katerina Nasioka, and Eloína Peláez for their comments on an earlier version. —J.H.

Index

"Passim" (literally "scattered") indicates intermittent discussion of a topic over a cluster of pages.

About the authors

Raoul Vaneigem was born in 1934 in Lessines, Belgium, a small town whose traditional claim to fame was the production of paving stones but which in the twentieth century also produced the Surrealist painter René Magritte and the Surrealist poet Louis Scutenaire. Vaneigem grew up in the wake of World War II in a working-class, socialist and anti-clerical milieu. He studied Romance philology at the Free University of Brussels and embarked on a teaching career that he later abandoned in favor of writing.

In late 1960 Vaneigem was introduced to Guy Debord by Henri Lefebvre, and soon afterward he joined the Situationist International, which Debord and his comrades-in-arms had founded in 1957. He was a leading light in the group throughout the 1960s.

Vaneigem is a prolific writer and a relentless critic of late capitalism. Among his works translated into English are *The Revolution of Everyday Life* (PM Press, 2012 [1967]); *The Totality for Kids* (Christopher Gray/Situationist International, 1966 ['Banalités de Base', 1962–63]); *Contributions to the Revolutionary Struggle* (Bratach Dubh, 1981 [*De la grève sauvage à l'autogestion généralisée*, 1974]); *A Cavalier History of Surrealism* (AK Press, 1999 [1977]); *The Book of Pleasures* (Pending Press, 1983 [1979]); *The Movement of the Free Spirit* (Zone Books, 1994 [1986]); and *A Declaration of the Rights of Human Beings* (PM Press, 2019 [2001]).

PM Press plans soon to publish two more titles: *The Knight, the Lady, the Devil, and Death* (2003) and *The Inhumanity of Religion* (2000).

John Holloway is a professor of sociology at the Instituto de Ciencias Sociales y Humanidades in the Benemérita Universidad Autónoma de Puebla, Mexico. His books include *We Are the Crisis of Capital: A John Holloway Reader* (2019); *Beyond Crisis: After the Collapse of Institutional Hope in Greece, What?* (2019); *In, Against, and Beyond Capitalism: The San Francisco Lectures* (2016); and *Change the World without Taking Power: The Meaning of Revolution Today* (2002).

The Translator

Donald Nicholson-Smith was born in Manchester, England, and is a longtime resident of New York City. Among his many translations are Raoul Vaneigem's *The Revolution of Everyday Life* (revised ed., PM Press, 2012), Guy Debord's *The Society of the Spectacle* (Zone, 2012), and *Guy Debord* by Anselm Jappe (PM Press, 2018).

ABOUT PM PRESS

PM Press was founded at the end of 2007 by a small collection of folks with decades of publishing, media, and organizing experience. PM Press co-conspirators have published and distributed hundreds of books, pamphlets, CDs, and DVDs. Members of PM have founded enduring book fairs, spearheaded victorious tenant organizing campaigns, and worked closely with bookstores, academic conferences, and even rock bands to deliver political and challenging ideas to all walks of life. We're old enough to know what we're doing and young enough to know what's at stake.

We seek to create radical and stimulating fiction and non-fiction books, pamphlets, T-shirts, visual and audio materials to entertain, educate, and inspire you. We aim to distribute these through every available channel with every available technology—whether that means you are seeing anarchist classics at our bookfair stalls, reading our latest vegan cookbook at the café, downloading geeky fiction e-books, or digging new music and timely videos from our website.

PM Press is always on the lookout for talented and skilled volunteers, artists, activists, and writers to work with. If you have a great idea for a project or can contribute in some way, please get in touch.

PM Press
PO Box 23912
Oakland, CA 94623
www.pmpress.org

PM Press in Europe
europe@pmpress.org
www.pmpress.org.uk

FRIENDS OF PM PRESS

These are indisputably momentous times—the
financial system is melting down globally and
the Empire is stumbling. Now more than ever
there is a vital need for radical ideas.

In the years since its founding—and on a
mere shoestring—PM Press has risen to the formidable challenge
of publishing and distributing knowledge and entertainment for the
struggles ahead. With over 300 releases to date, we have published an
impressive and stimulating array of literature, art, music, politics, and
culture. Using every available medium, we've succeeded in connecting
those hungry for ideas and information to those putting them into
practice.

Friends of PM allows you to directly help impact, amplify, and revitalize
the discourse and actions of radical writers, filmmakers, and artists. It
provides us with a stable foundation from which we can build upon our
early successes and provides a much-needed subsidy for the materials
that can't necessarily pay their own way. You can help make that
happen—and receive every new title automatically delivered to your
door once a month—by joining as a Friend of PM Press. And, we'll throw
in a free T-shirt when you sign up.

Here are your options:

- **$30 a month** Get all books and pamphlets plus 50% discount on all
  webstore purchases

- **$40 a month** Get all PM Press releases (including CDs and DVDs)
  plus 50% discount on all webstore purchases

- **$100 a month** Superstar—Everything plus PM merchandise, free
  downloads, and 50% discount on all webstore purchases

For those who can't afford $30 or more a month, we have **Sustainer
Rates** at $15, $10 and $5. Sustainers get a free PM Press T-shirt and a
50% discount on all purchases from our website.

Your Visa or Mastercard will be billed once a month, until you tell us to
stop. Or until our efforts succeed in bringing the revolution around. Or
the financial meltdown of Capital makes plastic redundant. Whichever
comes first.

The Revolution of Everyday Life

Raoul Vaneigem
Translated by Donald Nicholson-Smith

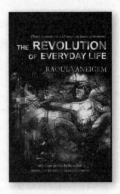

ISBN: 978-1-60486-678-0
$20.00   288 pages

Originally published just months before the May 1968 upheavals in France, Raoul Vaneigem's *The Revolution of Everyday Life* offered a lyrical and aphoristic critique of the "society of the spectacle" from the point of view of individual experience. Whereas Debord's masterful analysis of the new historical conditions that triggered the uprisings of the 1960s armed the revolutionaries of the time with theory, Vaneigem's book described their feelings of desperation directly, and armed them with "formulations capable of firing point-blank on our enemies."

"I realise," writes Vaneigem in his introduction, "that I have given subjective will an easy time in this book, but let no one reproach me for this without first considering the extent to which the objective conditions of the contemporary world advance the cause of subjectivity day after day."

Vaneigem names and defines the alienating features of everyday life in consumer society: survival rather than life, the call to sacrifice, the cultivation of false needs, the dictatorship of the commodity, subjection to social roles, and above all the replacement of God by the Economy. And in the second part of his book, "Reversal of Perspective," he explores the countervailing impulses that, in true dialectical fashion, persist within the deepest alienation: creativity, spontaneity, poetry, and the path from isolation to communication and participation.

For "To desire a different life is already that life in the making." And "fulfillment is expressed in the singular but conjugated in the plural."

The present English translation was first published by Rebel Press of London in 1983. This new edition of *The Revolution of Everyday Life* has been reviewed and corrected by the translator and contains a new preface addressed to English-language readers by Raoul Vaneigem.

A Declaration of the Rights of Human Beings: On the Sovereignty of Life as Surpassing the Rights of Man, Second Edition

Raoul Vaneigem

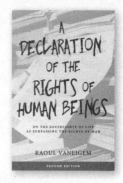

ISBN: 978-1-62963-155-4
$20.00   192 pages

"A declaration of rights is indispensable in order to halt the ravages of despotism." So wrote the revolutionary Antoine Barnave in support of the Declaration of the Rights of Man and of the Citizen (1789). Over two centuries after the Great French Revolution, Raoul Vaneigem writes that today, "in a situation comparable to the condition of France on the eve of its Revolution," we cannot limit ourselves to demanding liberties—the so-called bourgeois freedoms—that came into being with free trade, for now the free exchange of capital is the totalitarian form of a system which reduces human beings and the earth itself to merchandise. The time has come to give priority to the real individual rather than to Man in the abstract, the citizen answerable to the State and to the sole dictates of God's successor, the economy.

Sometimes playful or poetic, always provocative, Raoul Vaneigem reviews the history of bills of rights before offering his own call, with commentary, for fifty-seven rights yet to be won in a world where the "freedoms accorded to Man" are no longer merely "the freedoms accorded by man to the economy."

Every human being has the right, for example: to become human and to be treated as such; to dispose freely of their time; to comfort and luxury; to free modes of transport set up by and for the collectivity; to permanent control over scientific experimentation; to association by affinity; to bend toward life what was turned toward death; to a natural life and a natural death; to hold nothing sacred; to excess and to moderation; to desire what seems beyond the realm of the possible.

Readers of Vaneigem's now-classic work *The Revolution of Everyday Life* will find much to engage with in this unique work of subversive utopianism.

"All opponents of globalization should carry it in their luggage."
—*Le Monde*

In, Against, and Beyond Capitalism: The San Francisco Lectures

John Holloway
with a Preface by Andrej Grubačić

ISBN: 978-1-62963-109-7
$14.95   112 pages

In, Against, and Beyond Capitalism is based
on three recent lectures delivered by John
Holloway at the California Institute of Integral
Studies in San Francisco. The lectures focus on what anticapitalist
revolution can mean today—after the historic failure of the idea that
the conquest of state power was the key to radical change—and offer a
brilliant and engaging introduction to the central themes of Holloway's
work.

The lectures take as their central challenge the idea that "We Are the
Crisis of Capital and Proud of It." This runs counter to many leftist
assumptions that the capitalists are to blame for the crisis, or that crisis
is simply the expression of the bankruptcy of the system. The only way
to see crisis as the possible threshold to a better world is to understand
the failure of capitalism as the face of the push of our creative force. This
poses a theoretical challenge. The first lecture focuses on the meaning
of "We," the second on the understanding of capital as a system of
social cohesion that systematically frustrates our creative force, and the
third on the proposal that we are the crisis of this system of cohesion.

*"His Marxism is premised on another form of logic, one that affirms
movement, instability, and struggle. This is a movement of thought that
affirms the richness of life, particularity (non-identity) and 'walking in the
opposite direction'; walking, that is, away from exploitation, domination,
and classification. Without contradictory thinking in, against, and beyond
the capitalist society, capital once again becomes a reified object, a thing,
and not a social relation that signifies transformation of a useful and
creative activity (doing) into (abstract) labor. Only open dialectics, a right
kind of thinking for the wrong kind of world, non-unitary thinking without
guarantees, is able to assist us in our contradictory struggle for a world free
of contradiction."*
—Andrej Grubačić, from his Preface

"Holloway's work is infectiously optimistic."
—Steven Poole, the *Guardian* (UK)

We Are the Crisis of Capital: A John Holloway Reader

John Holloway

ISBN: 978-1-62963-225-4
$22.95   320 pages

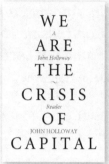

We Are the Crisis of Capital collects articles and excerpts written by radical academic, theorist, and activist John Holloway over a period of forty years.

Different times, different places, and the same anguish persists throughout our societies. This collection asks, "Is there a way out?" How do we break capital, a form of social organisation that dehumanises us and threatens to annihilate us completely? How do we create a world based on the mutual recognition of human dignity?

Holloway's work answers loudly, "By screaming NO!" By thinking from our own anger and from our own creativity. By trying to recover the "We" who are buried under the categories of capitalist thought. By opening the categories and discovering the antagonism they conceal, by discovering that behind the concepts of money, state, capital, crisis, and so on, there moves our resistance and rebellion.

An approach sometimes referred to as Open Marxism, it is an attempt to rethink Marxism as daily struggle. The articles move forward, influenced by the German state derivation debates of the seventies, by the CSE debates in Britain, and the group around the Edinburgh journal *Common Sense*, and then moving on to Mexico and the wonderful stimulus of the Zapatista uprising, and now the continuing whirl of discussion with colleagues and students in the Posgrado de Sociología of the Benemérita Universidad Autónoma de Puebla.

"Holloway's work is infectiously optimistic."
—Steven Poole, the *Guardian* (UK)

"Holloway's thesis is indeed important and worthy of notice."
—Richard J.F. Day, *Canadian Journal of Cultural Studies*

Guy Debord

Anselm Jappe
Translated by Donald Nicholson-
Smith, with a Foreword by T.J. Clark

ISBN: 978-1-62963-449-4
$21.95   224 pages

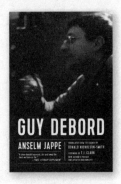

This is the first and best intellectual
biography of Guy Debord, prime mover of the
Situationist International (1957–1972) and
author of *The Society of the Spectacle*, perhaps
the seminal book of the May 1968 uprising in France. Anselm Jappe
offers a powerful corrective to the continual attempts to incorporate
Debord's theoretical work into "French theory." Jappe's focus, to the
contrary, is on Debord's debt to the Hegelian-Marxist tradition, to Karl
Korsch and Georg Lukács, and more generally to left-Marxist currents
of council communism. His close reading of Debord's magnum opus
supplies a superb gloss that has never been rivaled despite the great
flood of writing on the Situationists in recent decades.

At the same time, Debord is placed squarely in context among the
Letterist and Situationist anti-artists who, in the aftermath of World
War II, sought to criticize and transcend the legacy of Dada and
Surrealism. Jappe's book offers a lively account of the Situationists'
theory and practice as this "last avant-garde" made its way from radical
bohemianism to revolutionary theory and action.

Guy Debord has been translated into many languages. This PM Press
reprint edition benefits from a new author's preface and a bibliographical
update.

"A clear-headed account . . . far and away the best we have so far."
—*Times Literary Supplement*

*"The only book on Debord in either French or English that can be
unreservedly recommended . . . particularly useful for its extensive treatment
of the Marxian connection that is usually ignored in culture-oriented
accounts of the Situationists."*
—Ken Knabb, editor of *Situationist International Anthology*

Archive That, Comrade! Left Legacies and the Counter Culture of Remembrance

Phil Cohen

ISBN: 978-1-62963-506-4
$19.95   160 pages

Archive That, Comrade! explores issues of archival theory and practice that arise for any project aspiring to provide an open-access platform for political dialogue and democratic debate. It is informed by the author's experience of writing a memoir about his involvement in the London underground scene of the 1960s, the London street commune movement, and the occupation of 144 Piccadilly, an event that hit the world's headlines for ten days in July 1969.

After a brief introduction that sets the contemporary scene of 'archive fever,' the book considers what the political legacy of 1960s counter culture reveals about the process of commemoration. The argument then opens out to discuss the notion of historical legacy and its role in the 'dialectic of generations'. How far can the archive serve as a platform for dialogue and debate between different generations of activists in a culture that fetishises the evanescent present, practices a profound amnesia about its past, and forecloses the sociological imagination of an alternative future? The following section looks at the emergence of a complex apparatus of public fame and celebrity around the spectacle of dissidence and considers whether the Left has subverted or merely mirrored the dominant forms of reputation-making and public recognition. Can the Left establish its own autonomous model of commemoration? The final section takes up the challenge of outlining a model for the democratic archive as a revisionary project, creating a resource for building collective capacity to sustain struggles of long duration. A postscript examines how archival strategies of the alt-right have intervened at this juncture to elaborate a politics of false memory.

"Has the Left got a past? And if so, is that past best forgotten? Who was it who said, 'Let the dead bury their dead'? Phil Cohen's book is a searing meditation on the politics of memory, written by someone for whom 'the '60s' are still alive—and therefore horrible, unfinished, unforgivable, tremendous, undead. His book brings back to life the William Faulkner cliché. The past for Cohen is neither dead nor alive. It's not even past, more's the pity."
—T.J. Clark, author of *The Sight of Death*

Witches, Witch-Hunting, and Women

Silvia Federici

ISBN: 978-1-62963-568-2
$14.00   120 pages

We are witnessing a new surge of interpersonal and institutional violence against women, including new witch hunts. This surge of violence has occurred alongside an expansion of capitalist social relations. In this new work that revisits some of the main themes of *Caliban and the Witch*, Silvia Federici examines the root causes of these developments and outlines the consequences for the women affected and their communities. She argues that, no less than the witch hunts in sixteenth- and seventeenth-century Europe and the "New World," this new war on women is a structural element of the new forms of capitalist accumulation. These processes are founded on the destruction of people's most basic means of reproduction. Like at the dawn of capitalism, what we discover behind today's violence against women are processes of enclosure, land dispossession, and the remolding of women's reproductive activities and subjectivity.

As well as an investigation into the causes of this new violence, the book is also a feminist call to arms. Federici's work provides new ways of understanding the methods in which women are resisting victimization and offers a powerful reminder that reconstructing the memory of the past is crucial for the struggles of the present.

"It is good to think with Silvia Federici, whose clarity of analysis and passionate vision come through in essays that chronicle enclosure and dispossession, witch-hunting and other assaults against women, in the present, no less than the past. It is even better to act armed with her insights."
—Eileen Boris, Hull Professor of Feminist Studies, University of California, Santa Barbara

Eclipse and Re-emergence of the Communist Movement

Gilles Dauvé and François Martin

ISBN: 978-1-62963-043-4
$14.95   168 pages

In the years following 1968, a number of
people involved in the most radical aspects
of the French general strike felt the need to
reflect on their experiences and to relate them
to past revolutionary endeavors. This meant
studying previous attempts and theories, namely those of the post-1917
German-Dutch and Italian Communist Left. The original essays included
here were first written between 1969 and 1972 and circulated amongst
left communist and worker circles.

But France was not the only country where radicals sought to
contextualize their political environment and analyze their own radical
pasts. Over the years these three essays have been published separately
in various languages and printed as books in both the United States and
the UK with few changes. This third English edition is updated to take
into account the contemporary political situation; half of the present
volume is new material.

The book argues that doing away with wage-labor, class, the State, and
private property is necessary, possible, and can only be achieved by a
historical break, one that would certainly differ from October 1917 . . .
yet it would not be a peaceful, gradual, piecemeal evolution either. Like
their historical predecessors—Marx, Rosa Luxemburg, Anton Pannekoek,
Amadeo Bordiga, Durruti, and Debord—the authors maintain a belief in
revolution.

*"Gilles Dauvé is well-known in certain circles for his radical ideas about the
functioning of modern capitalist society. The author has had a significant
influence on both libertarian communists and anarchists."*
—Iš rankų į rankas press (Lithuania)

A Blaze in a Desert: Selected Poems

Victor Serge
Edited and translated by James
Brook with an Afterword by
Richard Greeman

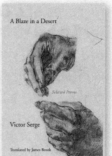

ISBN: 978-1-62963-382-4
$16.95   192 pages

Victor Serge (1890–1947) played many parts,
as he recounted in his indelible *Memoirs of a Revolutionary*. The son of
anti-czarist exiles in Brussels, Serge was a young anarchist in Paris; a
syndicalist rebel in Barcelona; a Bolshevik in Petrograd; a Comintern
agent in Central Europe; a comrade of Trotsky's; a friend of writers like
Andrei Bely, Boris Pilnyak, and André Breton; a prisoner of Stalin; a
dissident Marxist in exile in Mexico . . .

Like Serge's extraordinary novels, *A Blaze in a Desert: Selected Poems*
bears witness to decades of revolutionary upheavals in Europe and
the advent of totalitarian rule; many of the poems were written during
the "immense shipwreck" of Stalin's ascendancy. In poems datelined
Petrograd, Orenburg, Paris, Marseille, the Caribbean, and Mexico, Serge
composed elegies for the fallen—as well as prospective elegies for the
living who, like him, endured prison, exile, and bitter disappointment in
the revolutions of the first half of the twentieth century:

Night falls, the boat pulls in,
stop singing.
Exile relights its captive lamps
on the shore of time.

A Blaze in a Desert comprises Victor Serge's sole published book of
poetry, *Resistance* (1938), his unpublished manuscript *Messages* (1946),
and his last poem, "Hands" (1947).

*"Victor Serge was a major novelist, a revolutionary, and a historical witness,
so it is perhaps not surprising that his poetry has been overlooked. But his
poetry is for real. It is as grounded in specifics as you might expect from a
fighter in some of the twentieth century's great struggles, and as visionary
as you'd hope from a disciple of Rimbaud and a friend to the Surrealists.
Reading it is like coming upon an unsuspected corridor in the house of
literature. James Brook's lucid translation does it full justice."*
—Luc Sante, author of *The Other Paris* and translator of *Novels in Three
Lines* by Félix Fénéon

Pictures of a Gone City: Tech and the Dark Side of Prosperity in the San Francisco Bay Area

Richard A. Walker

ISBN: 978-1-62963-510-1
$26.95   480 pages

The San Francisco Bay Area is currently the jewel in the crown of capitalism—the tech capital of the world and a gusher of wealth from the Silicon Gold Rush. It has been generating jobs, spawning new innovation, and spreading ideas that are changing lives everywhere. It boasts of being the Left Coast, the Greenest City, and the best place for workers in the USA. So what could be wrong? It may seem that the Bay Area has the best of it in Trump's America, but there is a dark side of success: overheated bubbles and spectacular crashes; exploding inequality and millions of underpaid workers; a boiling housing crisis, mass displacement, and severe environmental damage; a delusional tech elite and complicity with the worst in American politics.

This sweeping account of the Bay Area in the age of the tech boom covers many bases. It begins with the phenomenal concentration of IT in Greater Silicon Valley, the fabulous economic growth of the bay region and the unbelievable wealth piling up for the 1% and high incomes of Upper Classes—in contrast to the fate of the working class and people of color earning poverty wages and struggling to keep their heads above water. The middle chapters survey the urban scene, including the greatest housing bubble in the United States, a metropolis exploding in every direction, and a geography turned inside out. Lastly, it hits the environmental impact of the boom, the fantastical ideology of Tech World, and the political implications of the tech-led transformation of the bay region.

"San Francisco has battened from its birth on instant wealth, high-tech weaponry, and global commerce, and the present age is little different. Gold, silver, and sleek iPhones—they all glitter in the California sun and are at least as magnetic as the city's spectacular setting, benign climate, and laissez-faire lifestyles. The cast of characters changes, but the hustlers and thought-shapers eternally reign over the city and its hinterland, while in their wake they leave a ruined landscape of exorbitant housing, suburban sprawl, traffic paralysis, and delusional ideas about a market free enough to rob the majority of their freedom. Read all about it here, and weep."
—Gray Brechin, author of *Imperial San Francisco: Urban Power, Earthly Ruin*